THE INTROVERTED PRESENTER

TEN STEPS FOR PREPARING AND DELIVERING SUCCESSFUL PRESENTATIONS

Richard Tierney

D1341169

Apress®

The Introverted Presenter: Ten Steps for Preparing and Delivering
Successful Presentations

Copyright © 2015 by **Richard Tierney**

ISBN-13 (pbk): 978-1-4842-1089-5

ISBN-13 (electronic): 978-1-4842-1088-8

Managing Director: Welmoed Spahr
Acquisitions Editor: Robert Hutchinson
Developmental Editor: Douglas Pundick
Editorial Board: Steve Anglin, Mark Beckner, Gary Cornell, Louise Corrigan, James DeWolf,
    Jonathan Gennick, Robert Hutchinson, Michelle Lowman, James Markham,
    Susan McDermott, Matthew Moodie, Jeffrey Pepper, Douglas Pundick, Ben Renow-Clarke,
    Gwenan Spearing, Matt Wade, Steve Weiss
Coordinating Editor: Rita Fernando
Copy Editor: Kim Wimpsett
Compositor: SPi Global
Indexer: SPi Global
Cover Designer: Friedhelm Steinen-Broo

Distributed to the book trade worldwide by Springer Science+Business Media New York, 233 Spring Street, 6th Floor, New York, NY 10013. Phone 1-800-SPRINGER, fax (201) 348-4505, e-mail orders-ny@springer-sbm.com, or visit www.springeronline.com. Apress Media, LLC is a California LLC and the sole member (owner) is Springer Science + Business Media Finance Inc (SSBM Finance Inc). SSBM Finance Inc is a Delaware corporation.

For information on translations, please e-mail rights@apress.com, or visit www.apress.com.

Apress and friends of ED books may be purchased in bulk for academic, corporate, or promotional use. eBook versions and licenses are also available for most titles. For more information, reference our Special Bulk Sales–eBook Licensing web page at www.apress.com/bulk-sales.

Any source code or other supplementary materials referenced by the author in this text is available to readers at www.apress.com. For detailed information about how to locate your book's source code, go to www.apress.com/source-code/.

Apress Business: The Unbiased Source of Business Information

Apress business books provide essential information and practical advice, each written for practitioners by recognized experts. Busy managers and professionals in all areas of the business world—and at all levels of technical sophistication—look to our books for the actionable ideas and tools they need to solve problems, update and enhance their professional skills, make their work lives easier, and capitalize on opportunity.

Whatever the topic on the business spectrum—entrepreneurship, finance, sales, marketing, management, regulation, information technology, among others—Apress has been praised for providing the objective information and unbiased advice you need to excel in your daily work life. Our authors have no axes to grind; they understand they have one job only—to deliver up-to-date, accurate information simply, concisely, and with deep insight that addresses the real needs of our readers.

It is increasingly hard to find information—whether in the news media, on the Internet, and now all too often in books—that is even-handed and has your best interests at heart. We therefore hope that you enjoy this book, which has been carefully crafted to meet our standards of quality and unbiased coverage.

We are always interested in your feedback or ideas for new titles. Perhaps you'd even like to write a book yourself. Whatever the case, reach out to us at editorial@apress.com and an editor will respond swiftly. Incidentally, at the back of this book, you will find a list of useful related titles. Please visit us at www.apress.com to sign up for newsletters and discounts on future purchases.

The Apress Business Team

*This book is dedicated to anyone
who has ever messed up a presentation.*

That's how we learn.

Contents

About the Author

Richard Tierney is a Presentation Coach with M62.com, an international presentation consultancy with offices in Singapore, Liverpool in the UK, and New York. Richard is also a coach at SupporTED, which provides coaching to the TED Fellows community.

He has 30 years of experience in over 20 countries as a business coach, innovation consultant, creative director, conference organizer, and media producer primarily in the IT, automotive, and consumer electronics sectors.

Despite being a congenital introvert, Tierney presents regularly at industry conferences in Europe and Asia. He was a council member of the British Association for Conferences and Events (ACE) and a member the British Academy of Film and Television Arts (BAFTA). Tierney has experience in theater and television and holds professional accreditations from London's Royal College of Art and London Business School.

Acknowledgments

This book would not have happened without all those "event tramps" I have had the pleasure to work with along the way in a career that has careened around the business that is show for many decades. You know who you are.

Mostly it is due to Katy Bird, who set me on this path without knowing she did so—and is sadly no longer with us to know what she did. Perhaps she does.

My wife, Fiona, is a tireless copy editor turning my random words into sense. She was ably succeeded by the terrific team at Apress, who can take comfort in their meager salaries. They surely deserve more, but Fiona didn't get paid at all. Perhaps she might.

My children are a constant source of inspiration and were so excited that they might go to a book launch. Perhaps they might.

Introduction

If you bought this book for a presentation you need to give right now, go straight to Chapter 13 and come back here when it's over.

For the rest of us who have more time, read on.

There are those naturals. They always get asked to speak because they love it. Because they love it, they seek it, and because they seek it, they become better at it.

Then there are the rest of us. We hate the spotlight and run away from it. We never get asked because we never volunteer. We never volunteer because we don't like it. So, we never improve.

We just get very good at procrastination.

We put off speaking, and we put off anything about presenting. We put off writing the speech, we put off preparing the slides, and we put off rehearsals. And that makes us worse, which makes us hate it more.

This ends now. You may not like it, but you can do it. And if you do it, you may even come to like it.

Who knew?

Introverts and Presentations

Harnessing Terror

There are lots of presenting help books out there, so why should you read this one? If you too are an introvert, then this chapter explains why.

An introvert will always need support when making presentations. It's simply not in our nature to stand in front of an audience and speak. We can do it, but it's draining.

As you'll see, Jung first named us *introverts* because we draw our energy from the outside *inward*. Pushing energy outward is just not in our nature, and while this book will teach you a process by which you can shine on the speaker's platform, it will always leave you more exhausted than an extrovert.

The point is not to become an extrovert; that's not possible. The point is to acknowledge our makeup and evolve accordingly. And one of the most important things for introverts to get right is the structure and content of the presentation.

An extrovert giving a badly structured presentation will not do well, and an introvert will do just as badly but will feel much worse when doing it. So, it's much more important for an introvert to be well prepared. My promise to you is that if you follow the guidelines I have laid out here, you will make great presentations, and you'll have fun doing it. By following the guidelines in this book, you will get better and better because you'll understand what you're good at and have coping strategies for what you're not suited to do.

Here's the alternative scenario. An accomplished professional speaker—let's call him Dave—gives a great presentation at the company's annual conference. Mary, a salesperson in the audience, admires his stage presence and wants to emulate him. She does a search online and—guess what!—Dave has written a "how-to" book sharing his personal secrets and tips for presenting. So, Mary buys it.

Late into the night she studies Dave's secrets, puts all he says into practice, and discovers that it does not work for her.

The reason is simple: Dave is an extrovert. From an early age he has been the star of the show; he's always the one who volunteers to be part of the nativity play, speech day, college debating society, and so on. That's why he's a presenter and speaker—he was born to do it. No matter how often Mary reads the book, she's missing a vital part. Mary is an introvert so will still dread getting up to speak no matter how many books like Dave's she reads.

The Introverted Presenter addresses this by leading you through the terror to a place of comfort and acceptance. Mary will never be a stand-up comic, but she can learn to present carefully prepared material her audience will connect with, and she can enjoy doing it.

I know this because I'm an introvert just like you.

About Me

When I was at school, about 13, I was asked to stand in front of the class and speak. My mystified classmates saw me standing, wordless. My vision went red and then green; next I passed out. Teenage boys are vicious in the face of weakness, but no one mentioned it, and I was never asked to stand and speak again. My *limiting belief*, established that day, was that I could never make a speech.

My career took me into theater, concert, and television production. Always backstage or behind the camera, I was privileged to work with some of the biggest names in the performing world. I watched the way great pop stars connected with their audience, learned from seeing one of our greatest actors rehearse one of his West End appearances, and enjoyed the seemingly end-less rehearsals famous directors spent on small, important pieces of stage direction.

You could always spot me in the audience; I was the one spending only half my time watching the stage. I was looking to see how the performance was received, as well as the techniques of those on stage—all refreshingly nervous backstage.

I then worked in company events and corporate video. I found that I could help inexperienced presenters feel relaxed, hone their content, and become more effective. Over the years I got better and better at doing this. I have worked with main board directors of more than 60 of the Fortune 100 companies, as well as with leading charities and small Internet startups.

I have coached those making presentations in more than 30 countries, from a deserted Indonesian island to five-star conference centers and Buckingham Palace, from CEOs to disadvantaged children. I'm trained in neurolinguistic programming (NLP), theater, film, business, and mentoring.

About five years ago I started my own consultancy and needed to demonstrate that I was an expert in the field. With a sinking heart, I realized that this meant I must volunteer to speak at industry events. I employed all that I had—unwittingly—learned through my career in the United Kingdom, in Europe, and further afield at more than 60 engagements globally. It worked. I proved what I'd always suspected: that to become successful in any field, you must be a confident speaker, and that my limiting belief was based in myth. I recognized myself as an introvert and trained myself to speak, and I'm now going to tell you how to as well.

Feared More Than Death

Destroying Some Myths

There's a "survey" quoted by almost all presentation training companies. The gist of it is that when people are asked what they fear most, public speaking is the highest out of all the replies. It's higher than death, which is number two. This supposedly academic piece of research is used by most trainers to say "At a funeral, would you really rather be in the coffin instead of reading the eulogy?" In fact, I can find no evidence that the survey really exists. There are a lot of these surveys that are regularly trotted out by professional speakers; most are pure invention, but they put some pseudo-academic veracity to a universal truth, usually the result of a dinner conversation made credible.

Before going further, I have to break some news to you: we are all going to die. As the Russians say, "Life is dangerous; no one has survived it yet." So, if you ask what people most fear in their lives, death is kind of a given. No wonder the fictitious respondents focus on the things that will happen before the inevitable.

The truth supported by this invention is that most people are afraid of standing up in public because most people are introverts. My Myers Briggs type is INFP. The important thing here is that the first letter is an *I*. The choice is *I* or *E*: introvert or extrovert. More than 50 percent of us are *I*. Sources differ in their percentages, but everyone agrees that more people are introverted rather than extroverted.

The Myers-Briggs Type Indicator (MBTI) assessment is a psychometric questionnaire designed to measure preferences in how people perceive the world and make decisions. These preferences were extrapolated from the theories of Carl Jung first published in 1921.

Created by Katherine Cook Briggs and her daughter, Isabel Briggs Meyers, the test was designed to help women entering work for the first time. The initial questionnaire grew into the Myers-Briggs Type Indicator, which was first published in 1962.

CPP, Inc., the publisher of the MBTI instrument, calls it "the world's most widely used personality assessment" with as many as 2 million assessments administered annually.

The test plots an individual's preferences on four "dichotomies," or preferences:

Extroversion (E) versus Introversion (I)

Sensing (S) versus Intuition (N)

Thinking (T) versus Feeling (F)

Judgment (J) versus Perception (P)

The four-letter Meyers Briggs types (intuition is represented by an N) are not indicators of aptitude, only preference. It's easy to slip into some mistakes because, for example, if you were given a high judgment score, it does not mean you are necessarily judgmental.

When it comes to public speakers, such as the ones who are on TV night after night and the ones who earn the big bucks from their performances, they are mostly extroverts. They are the ones in short supply. It's nothing more complex than supply and demand. People who are good at public speaking are in the minority and therefore get well paid.

Those great speakers are genetically programmed to be good at it. At school they always took the lead in the play, they went on to college and chaired the debating society, everyone invites them to be the best man or woman at their wedding because the speeches are so amusing, at work they fly because they always look impressive when presenting, they are great salespeople, and they actively seek the limelight. We'll have nothing to do with them because they are not like us. To perform the way they perform, we need different strategies and better support.

Yet we mere mortals look at an extrovert's suave competence and expect to do the same. They don't seem to prepare much, so we don't; they tell jokes well, so we try to do the same; and they get applause, so we wonder why we don't.

I'm doing alright for a bloke of my age, but I don't try to compete against Olympic athletes, bodybuilders, or male models. I need a different strategy, and if you have picked up this book, you have recognized that you too need a different strategy to shine on the podium. You need a strategy suited to you, an *introverted* presenter.

Here's the second bit of news: to give an effective presentation, you'll have to expose a bit of yourself and give away a bit of your personality. We introverts hate that, but remember the last great talk you heard. The presenter didn't just report the bare facts; the presenter made it personal. It was personal to the audience but also personal to their experience. Otherwise, it has no resonance. Think about why you went to the last performance you attended; it's not because you wanted to hear a monotone rendition of your favorite text. It's because you wanted to see a great interpretation of the work. I had an English teacher who made Shakespeare sound dull. I now realize that it's because he was bored with teaching. I'm glad to say I've seen and worked with many actors who showed me how Shakespeare can sound interesting.

I think we can all acknowledge what actors are taught: that when an actor truly inhabits the emotions of the part, then the communication of the story becomes transcendental. If you think back to the last play, film, or TV show you saw, I bet you can't remember every word of the script, but I bet you can remember how you felt at the end. In fact, there is recent research showing that audience members remember their feeling watching a performance and then adjust their memories of the production to make the memory match the emotion. It's not the other way around.

One thing introverts hate is revealing their feelings to a large group. To be an effective presenter, you need to be prepared to reveal your feelings and to use them in making the speech. You'll hate it, but it will work. I'll let that thought settle with you as we work through the process, and I hope you won't be too shocked when we get to that part.

Draw faith from the fact you have picked up this book and that you acknowledge who and what you are. Trust that I have managed to give effective presentations on many occasions despite being—just like you—an introvert and that there are many ways you can shine when you deliver using the kind of preparation I can tell you about.

Let's get started. The next chapter takes you on the first step in the method I have developed to prepare presentations you can enjoy giving.

Before you turn the page, if you want, take a look at IntrovertedPreseter.com, where I have put a page of links to examples of great presentations, and look at the Introverted Presenter Facebook pages. Take a look at the links to TED. com, which contains some of the most inspiring presentations I have seen. The presentations I have chosen are all examples of how introverts can shine through clarity and preparation. Beware that once you take a look at TED.com, you may never escape!

MARY'S JOURNEY BEGINS: THE INITIAL PANIC

Mary had just been promoted to the giddy heights of submanager in the Financial Services Company where she has worked for three years. From her slightly bigger desk, she can actually see daylight at times; she has an assistant for the first time in her life and struggles to find enough things for her to do.

It's Tuesday morning, and her manager tells her about the association conference in Birmingham. The event contains a number of presentations by individual companies reviewing developments in the past year. Traditionally these presentations have been made by staff at Mary's level. Her predecessor always gave great presentations. Would Mary have her presentation slides on his desk in ten days?

Mary starts to panic. She didn't realize that her new post meant she'd have to give speeches!

The rest of Tuesday and Wednesday go by in a blur. Yes, she's doing all the things she's paid to do but in a disengaged manner. Her every moment is filled with the desire to not think about the speech. She hates giving presentations and would certainly not have accepted the promotion if she'd known. No one at work can know how much she's panicking.

Wednesday evening comes, and she's meeting some friends from college. The stress is starting to get to her. She drinks too much and indulges in a little alcohol-fuelled honesty.

Thursday morning arrives, and through a searing headache Mary sees an e-mail from one friend who was at the pub the night before. Mike was also afraid to give presentations, and he too was held back in his career, so he offers to help her. Oh, and he promises to keep what she'd like to do to Ryan Gosling to himself.

The first step, Mike tells Mary, is to understand that she can do this. She has an above-average intelligence, and lots of people get through presentations without disaster occurring, even if they are not "natural" speakers. It may not be her favorite thing to do, but she does lots of things she does not like. The first thing is to accept that she's going to give this presentation and that she needs to use all her skills to prepare. Ignoring it is not an option and will only make it worse. Mike promises to be in touch in a few days to ask her about what she has to do.

Immediately Mary feels less anxious. There's now a date when she will deal with the presentation, and she feels there's nothing to be done right away. While she's still scared, she takes solace from the knowledge that Mike has faced this devil and survived. In the following days, she is at least able to cope with the other parts of her workload and actually think about something other than her impending doom.

Your Objective

The First Step

I'm assuming you are reading this book because you have a presentation in mind. If you follow my method, it will also set the template to allow you to not just give one great presentation but also follow a path with a set of tools that allow you to shine in the future. Each time you use this process you will build on the time before. The first step on that journey is your presentation that we will work through together—the one that's on your mind right now. This is the start of the process I use every time I give a presentation. If I am feeling over-confident or, worse, lazy, I occasionally skip a step. It always comes back to haunt me later. So, here is step 1.

Step 1: Define Your Audience

I want you to start preparing yourself by thinking about the event and your audience. Write down (I know, it's not very cool, and you don't want someone coming across your notes, but just do it because this is important) everything you know about the audience you will be presenting to. Write down the age range, the demographics, whether they are known to you, how they can influence your future, how much they earn, how much you care about them, everything. If you're not sure, make your best guess. It's just between you and a piece of paper you are going to eat soon anyway.

Once you have defined everything you know about the audience, then ask this question: what state is your audience in when you think about your presentation? What I mean is, what is their knowledge, emotional attachment, and attitude? For example, how would you rate them in knowledge, positivity, motivation, and openness?

I was once asked to advise one of the U.K. utility companies on making its presentations more creative. When I examined the personality traits of the group I was working with, I realized that in a heavily regulated environment the recruitment function effectively screened out anyone who might have wanted to think outside a very limited brief. These people essentially wanted to be told what to do. So, my client did just that. To treat them any other way would have required a lot more time and—I believe—would have been unpleasant for them and unproductive for the speaker. Know your audience, and always respect who and where they are.

These two statements of your audience—description and state—are separate and important pieces of information. Keep them in mind because I'll be referring to them throughout the process. The information is important in terms of content, whether we need to persuade or inform, and in terms of tone; you would not speak to your child the same way you might speak to your boss. For now we are going to focus on the first use for the information.

Now that you know all you can know about the audience you will be facing, answer this question: what do you want your audience to do once your presentation is over? Get that clear in your mind.

There are lots of things in the way of this clarity, and what gets in the way here is why you have been asked to speak. For example, it may be a speech that your boss gave last year, and now he can't be bothered to repeat the process, so you have to do it. But whatever the reason for you being lumbered with this task and whatever the reason for this audience being assembled in front of you, I want you to put that out of your mind when considering how you want this audience to behave. The reason you are there is irrelevant, truly.

There is only one thing that matters at this point in the process of making you a happy presenter. What can this group of individuals do for you? This thinking is often called *zero-base planning*, and it's useful in a lot of business process reengineering. We essentially ask the question, "If I had to start from nothing, what would I do?" I'm sure you can think of instances where business decisions are made on the basis of previous experience plus inflation, or some other adjustment.

So, to bring it back to your presentation, the worst thing you can do is a DILLY. Some years ago I was working with a lighting designer called Gus Stewart on an annual conference for an IT multinational company. I was explaining the requirements of the meeting, and he said, "So, it's a DILLY job?" It was an expression I'd never heard before, so Gus had to explain. "Do. It. Like. Last. Year."

DILLY should be something you avoid at all costs. If you find yourself referencing the last time this presentation slot was filled, you will produce something that is boring and repetitive.

The audience you have can do something for you. This is what a presentation is all about. It is your chance to ask and influence them to take action. What is the most useful thing they can do for you? Think long and hard about this; it's your golden opportunity.

Be really specific. What do you want your audience to do specifically, in what timescale? What exact action? How often? To whom? Write this down several times, refining each time you do. Your objective is to reduce the action you desire to a really pithy statement that will fit on a sticky note; it will fit if you are specific enough. Finally, make a neat version you can place somewhere within clear sight while we finish the process of preparing your presentation. This action statement is a vital part of our progress.

Now go to bed.

In the morning, if you spot any generalization in your sticky note, then you need to do more work. For example, "To engender a positive image for the project among the wider stakeholders" will not do. What we are looking for is "More than 50 percent of the audience to contact us for a quote within 14 days." See what I mean? Specific.

Because we are introverts, there's a mechanism that seems to kick in regularly. As any step in the process becomes tricky, we start to question why it's us giving the presentation. Your mind is working overtime trying to find reasons why Sally from account management should be speaking in your place. This is a completely understandable defense mechanism. Understandable as it may be, the effect is to divert you from focusing on step of the process we are working with and send your mind on great loops of logic. I have constructed my process to make each part a small step that you can focus on to the exclusion of others. So, keep your head down, and don't let diversions interrupt the process. I know it works, and for now I just need you to trust.

I assure you this is the foundation for everything we are going to do together. It's as important as the foundation of the house you live in. It's never thought about after the building work is completed, yet it has a vital influence on your future well-being. So, go around this many times. Talk to anyone you can make sit still (buying drinks works well) and bore everyone to death with this until you feel you have a really concise action that your audience will be able to take in the time while they still remember you.

Having written the end objective for the presentation, the next stage is to move to a draft of the written text, and there are two steps to take to make you able to do that, which I'll cover in the next two chapters.

MARY FINDS HER FOCUS: IT'S NOT WHAT YOU KNOW

Three days later, and Mary's inbox makes that irritating "ping" noise: there's Mike. "Have not forgotten about you—tell me about this presentation."

"Oh, it's terrible," she writes, "25 minutes in front of the big-wigs from all the companies in our sector, and I have to say what I've done that is innovative…and I have not done anything innovative at all."

"Calm down," replies Mike, "you don't have to say what they tell you to say, and I'm sure you've done more than you think you have. Tell me all about it."

Mary spends the next 45 minutes writing, rewriting, editing, and thinking of more things to say. At the end she has written five pages of notes on the event, the reason she's there, the great slides her predecessor used, and how much she hates even the thought of doing it.

Mike replies, offering to meet her for a coffee the next day. In the meantime, he asks her to think about what she wants from the presentation and how she wants it to go—"… and being sick so you can't attend isn't an option."

After another sleepless night, Mary turns up looking less than perky.

"So, what have you discovered?" asks Mike.

"That I haven't got a clue, that I'm going to look awful, that I wish I could go back to my last job where I didn't earn as much money but didn't spend so much on trying to look perfect, and that this presentation is going to cost me a fortune in new clothes," Mary wailed into her latte.

Mike took a look at her notes. "It seems to me there's a lot of stuff in here that isn't really where you need to apply your mind at the moment. These are all important things to consider, but you need to decide what's important right now."

"Slides?" Mary asks.

"Not really," explains Mike. He takes a highlighter pen and starts scribbling on the notes. "I think there are two things to think about first: the people you'll be talking to and what you want from them." From these notes it seems to me that you have an opportunity to promote yourself to the other companies in your business, so that's personal networking, and you have an opportunity to sell your company's expertise, which might lead to some cross-industry sales. I think you have a personal objective and a corporate one."

They spent the next ten minutes arguing about all the other things that Mary felt were important. The majority of this time was spent on the slides. She had seen the slides her predecessor had used the previous year; Mary wanted slides that were impressive, but Mike was implacable. He gently persuaded Mary to focus on the objective of her presentation. Mike then asked her to write the five steps that led from her audience not knowing anything about her to understanding Mary's objective.

"Sorry, Mary, look at the time. I've got to dash. Catch you later," and he was gone.

Mary walked slowly back to the office mulling over what they'd discussed. She still wasn't sure Mike had the answers, but he surely had more of a clue than she did.

At her desk an e-mail popped up:

Mare

Sorry I had to leave.

Write those steps down and let's talk again.

   M x

That night she slept well for the first time since being given the task. She felt she was not alone in this and someone was pointing her in the right direction.

Presentation Structure

Building Your Road Map

Having established the action your audience should take at the end of your presentation, you now have a destination for your speech. It's a bit like driving a car; if we simply took the most attractive turn at each junction, we would never reach a chosen destination. You now have a way to structure the presentation that will make your audience feel confident that you know what you're doing. Because you do.

The story you are about to tell needs a start (where the audience is right now) and an end (your destination). When I asked you to define your audience, I also asked where they were in relation to your topic.

To recap, the definition of your audience defines the tone of your presentation, and the definition of their state is going to help us structure the presentation.

It's a journey from where the audience might be at the moment to where you want them to be in order to take the action you are demanding at the end of your presentation. There are two ways to do this: the lecture way and the story way. I'll describe the lecture way first.

When I call a structure the lecture version, it's because this is the structure used in—naturally—most teaching environments, and it is the structure of almost every training package I've seen. A bit like a game of chess, it's simple to describe, yet you can spend a lifetime learning how to use all the possible permutations available.

There's a well-known show business adage called the *rule of three*. Stand-up comics will always put their weakest joke at the end of a group of three because if you tell three jokes in a row, the last one will always get the biggest laugh; politicians deliver their statements in groups of three in the knowledge that the third statement will get the round of applause. You can find groups of three in Shakespeare, Moliere, and even the Bible. It's a powerful way to communicate.

Simply write three statements that take your audience from where they are at the moment to where you want them to be; then for each of the three points, make three subpoints. Now your structure is as follows: at the beginning of your presentation, you simply tell the audience a brief version of the three things you are going to tell them, then you go through all three in detail illustrating with the three subpoints, and finally you end by reviewing the three points and concluding with your "what to do" statement.

It's often described as tell them what you're going to tell them, tell them, and then tell them what you told them. It sounds a bit bald when described the way I've done here, but with a bit of subtlety it is effective and might be right for you.

The story version is a different way to approach a presentation and might be more appropriate for your needs. The story method is, um, a story. Humans are made to tell one another stories; it's what we do in the playground, it's what we do around the watercooler, it's what we do at home, and it's what we do to attract and keep a mate. It's sometimes more difficult to make a presentation work this way, but if you can, the emotional attachment is much greater because your audience will feel you have shared a little of yourself in the process. As introverts, we therefore steer away from this on the platform, but since we actually would communicate this way in other situations, it can be a way for an introvert to shine.

The tricky part is finding the right story. You are looking for as personal a tale as possible, which again takes the audience through the journey from where they are at the moment to the action you want them to take. We introverts tend to steer away from personal revelation, but once we've turned that corner, you will find that telling the story is actually easier than delivering a lecture. This is because it's a personal story, and we never have trouble answering questions like "How was your journey?" or "Did you find us alright?" We are also less likely to forget where we are in the story because it's obvious and sequential. So, take some time to consider all the options.

Either way, the step you need to complete is finding the logical sequence of steps that take you from the beginning of your presentation to the end action statement. Whichever you choose, write it down before we move on to the next step.

Some years ago I was trying to sell a historical documentary to a U.K. broadcaster. The broadcaster didn't seem interested, so my pitch was clearly not perfect. In expressing my frustration, I spoke to a screenwriting friend. I explained that I was really fired up about this fantastic story and could not understand why the commissioning editor at the broadcaster did not share my enthusiasm. The screenwriter responded by suggesting that instead of making a historical documentary, I should propose a historical drama. Dramas are much more expensive (around five times the cost), but they generate a much larger audience (about 20 times if you get it right), and therefore the broadcaster might be prepared to stump up for that. The broadcaster didn't like that idea either, but I realized that particularly when dealing with material that is not very visual, a re-creation would be much more engaging. It would then become a personal story. That started me thinking about movies I have enjoyed that bring the past to life through telling personal stories. Personal stories are much more engaging than a text book, which is why I urge you to take the story route if you possibly can.

In the same way, it's difficult to explain in a presentation the ins and outs of a pensions fund, a research project, or anything intangible in nature, so in those cases, a personal story of the effect of the thing you are trying to illustrate is much more accessible than a dry list of facts.

Also, we should consider what makes a "good" presentation. Some think that the end of a good speech is when everyone in the audience nods sagely, strokes their chins, and makes their way to the coffee break in an orderly manner. I disagree. I think the end of a great presentation is when a substantial number of the audience members rush the stage demanding more information or taking issue with something the speaker has said.

Is this something introverts actively seek out? You bet we don't. We want everything nice and calm and nonconfrontational. But for the purposes of creating your presentation, I suggest you consider being just a bit provocative—something we'll come to in the next chapter—and that you think more about your "what I want them to do" statement that is the end of your script.

Let's consider for a moment what presentations are good at and what they do badly. When you see a presentation, you get a sense of who the person is, what they believe in, and how they view the world. What they do badly is to convey specific facts (unless there's only one of them) and convey dense information. What presentations are great at is conveying enthusiasm and putting your audience in the mood to find out more. So, do use this part of the process to identify links you can use to resources online that can back up your presentation. You can put these links in a handout, on your profile in the program, or on material in the reception and catering areas. This is one way to lengthen the life span of your message.

Incidentally, you might be able to hire someone else to write the presentation for you. If you do that, you still need to go through the process up to this point before you are in a position to brief a writer. A good writer, and there are some very good ones, cannot tell you what story you want to tell or what you want the audience to do at the end of your presentation. They all have strategies both subtle and overt to extract the information from you. The end result will be only as good as your brief, and up to this point all we've been defining the parameters of the presentation. In the next chapter, we'll look at the work of writing your presentation—assuming that you are going to do it yourself.

MARY STARTS TO FEEL IN CONTROL: GENTLE STEPS

Mary arrived at work the next day to another e-mail from Mike:

> *M. Where is it?*
>
> *M*

Cheeky Bugger she thought, but actually when she started writing, Mary found the words flowed easily. Within ten minutes she had an outline written and pinged back to Mike. She turned to the rest of her work without giving the presentation another thought for the next three hours.

After lunch there was a call. "Well done for doing that," Mike said, "but I don't think it's quite there." Mary fumed.

"But I thought that was what you wanted?"

"Well, it's the first step in what I wanted, but it doesn't really tell the story," said Mike. "Take another look at it and tell me what you think." Mary sat and ground her teeth for a while, and then she took a deep breath.

Mary printed out the list and read it again. She went to fetch a drink and read it some more, and then she started jotting notes on it. After 20 minutes she had a paper covered in scribbles, so she turned back to her computer and made a tidy version. She e-mailed it to Mike with a sarcastic comment about dictators, perfectionists, and whether Mike's parents were actually married when they had him.

An e-mail pinged back:

> *Pino Grigio? 6:30? M*

In the wine bar, Mary sipped her "attitude adjustor" as Mike looked over the new list. Then he put it to one side and—shouting over the music of Rihanna—said, "Why don't you just tell me what this is really about?" Mary replied in three short sentences. Mike made notes. He passed the paper back to her. "There's your outline. It's a story now. Another glass, or shall we get a bottle?"

Mike. Don't do that again. Thanks for the advice. My head hurts.

M x

Mary struggled through the next morning, and when she finally got around to the wine-stained piece of paper, she had difficulty making it all out, so she wrote up what she could understand and made up the rest. Then she rewrote the story of her presentation. Small parts of it started to sound like actual words a real speaker might use. She e-mailed the result to Mike and headed out to lunch with some work friends.

Writing Your Speech

The Work Can Begin

So, now you have it: a concise objective written on a sticky note and stuck where you can't fail to see it. Now it's time to write a script.

"What?"

Yes. Write a script.

"But I thought you did the slides first!"

Nope. Write a script. We will certainly come to slides in due course. But they come later; you may ask why.

"OK, why?

Well, slides are there to illustrate what you are trying to communicate, and indeed they have a big influence on how you are remembered. But they are support for your message. They are not the message.

"But Bill from accounts had great slides at the last company event."

Yes, he did, and you'll have great slides too; we're just not going to work on them now. At this point (and indeed every other point), introverts like to indulge in diversion activity because they rightly fear that actually writing the script will reveal something about themselves. They are right; it does. But (imagine Simon Cowell speaking here), you know what? That's what your audience showed up for. You. So, if you are going to reveal something about yourself, let's do it here where it's nice and safe with time to edit and adjust before we get to displaying it in all its glory in public. Yes, I know you were scared when I said the *P* word.

It's all about you and your words. So, let's take a little diversion before doing that.

"Thank you, I was looking for a little diversion."

I know. I was too.

When actors study at drama school, they spend a lot of time on their physical fitness because standing up in public is stressful. That's also why theater management spends so much money backstage on wardrobe care and remakes. Even the most professional accomplished actor leaves the stage drenched in sweat. Sorry, but it's true.

The reason is that they put everything into their performance; they focus on every nuance of the text to produce the best response they can get from their audience. So you, and I, who are unnatural performers, will be in a state of panic when we present. We will need every ounce of brain power just to stay upright speaking coherently. I don't mean to add to your panic, but that's the reality. So, you need everything that can be taken care of to be put in place before you reach the podium. This is my aim in taking you through this process: to be as calm as you can be under fire. Note the "as you can be" part.

That's why we take time here to get everything as well prepared as it can be.

"But how will I remember the script?"

Don't worry about that now. Just write the damn thing. OK, I have one more diversion for you before you start work.

"Thank you."

You're welcome.

When I was at film school, one of my tutors was Michael Bukht, who was also known as Michael Barry, the Crafty Cook, on radio and television in the UK; if you're older than 40, you might remember him. He taught me all I needed to know about writing for speech, which is different from writing anything else. As Michael said, "Sentences without verbs, OK!"

In fact, Michael didn't write his scripts; he dictated them to a secretary (remember them?) so he wasn't hung up by how the words looked on the page. If you want to emulate him, use a Dictaphone and then transcribe your own words. Almost any phone can do this now.

As a fledgling TV producer, one of the first jobs I was given was transcribing interviews before edits. I had to write down exactly what an interviewee said—not what they meant, what they said. We needed to know which words we had captured and could use in the edit. In transcribing these words, I saw how inaccurately we all use words, and even my basic knowledge of grammar was outraged by how blatant the mistakes looked when they were written on paper.

Try this for yourself. Go out for drinks with friends and listen. Really listen to what they literally say. As the evening goes on (and they drink more), the amount of grammatically inaccurate stuff that comes out of their mouths is fantastic. But we all understand what our mates are saying, so what's the problem?

The problem is lawyer-speak, which is taking over our lives. This is a *bête noir* of mine, so excuse me if I rant a bit here. Look at any sign anywhere, and you'll find it's not as we speak; it's how company lawyers try to mitigate liability. "Management are not responsible for damage occurring to private property residing in this storage facility" is not how we speak to one another as sentient human beings, and yet this kind of vocabulary and sentence construction is creeping into our lives. And guess who is leading the standard for lawyer-speak into battle? That's right, us introverts. We need to overcome our natural tendencies. Introverts like to hide behind conditions. We don't like confrontation, and speaking plainly can feel like that. Here's a chance to put all that behind you.

Finally, remember this is only the first draft. Once you have produced some text, we are going to spend some time working on it, refining it, and making it the best script you can have. So, don't worry that these words are going to be exactly what you will say. It will be much better than that.

Enough diversions. Here's exactly what we will do. First open your word processor on your computer and write the words on which you are going to end—your action statement at the end of the document. In front of that you are going to write your script with the knowledge of exactly where you are going.

Whichever structure you decided on in the previous chapter goes in front of this. Now you have a full presentation; it's just lacking the words you will actually say. If you feel confident, just start writing those words in right away; if you are a little hesitant—as we introverts are—then a technique I use is to take each part of the structure and turn that into a longer sentence and then take each of those sentences and make them three sentences, and so on, until you have all the information you require in place.

Do it quickly and don't think about it too much. We are attempting to get a first full draft down on paper in a way that we can work with it as we move toward your presentation. Once you have something written, we can begin the process of improving and refining it. I have known brilliant writers who can put 95 percent of the finished presentation down at this stage, and I have known situations where not one word of the first draft was in the final delivered speech.

And unless you think this is because you are inexperienced, I once had the privilege of speaking with Randy Nelson at Pixar. He told me that when they were producing *Finding Nemo*, the company and its artistic director John Lassiter spent five years refining the script for the movie before they commenced production. They believed that they had the perfect story laid out in the best possible way so that production would be a simple process of letting their brilliant animators put the images on the screen. Randy's guess was that only 20 percent of that original script actually ended up in the movie. This is because Pixar has the most impressive system for refining and improving its productions that results in its enviable cabinet full of Oscars and a hit rate of box-office successes that outshines anyone in Hollywood. So, if it's good enough for animated fish that earn millions of dollars worldwide, then it's good enough for you.

If you still need another diversion, I recommend timetowrite.com written by Jurgen Wolff who has lots of advice on writing, and also you can spend time signing up for his newsletter, which allows you to spend more time downloading his "overcome procrastination" report, which is something to do instead of facing up to the writing you have to do now.

I mean it. Now.

MARY GETS SCARED AGAIN: DON'T LOSE FAITH

Lunch was a sandwich in the local park. Mary's friends asked about the presentation: wasn't she scared? She admitted she was a little more than frightened and told them of Mike's help. "Who's Mike?" they all asked. "He works nearby, and he was in my class at college."

"He seems to be helping a lot."

"Yes, he is."

"So, he just happens to be nearby? He just happens to be helpful?"

"What?"

"Just saying."

Back at the office Mary looks at her outline again and starts doodling on the sheet. She starts drawing pictures that might be slides. The phone rings; it's Mike. He asks how she feels about writing the speech now. Mary is panicked.

"What? I don't need to write a script, do I? The outline is OK. I can just talk around the subject. I've started on my slides."

"You need to write a script, and I'll tell you how. I can explain why, but it's better to see what I mean. What are you doing this evening? Fancy seeing a movie?"

Mary is confused but flattered by the attention. "How will that help?"

"You'll be inspired by the way professional storytellers work."

The next morning she composes an e-mail:

> Mike
>
> *That was a lovely evening, but I don't see how a story of a love affair in the 1920s helps me sell financial services. What do I do with the presentation outline now?*
>
> *Great Italian by the way...*
>
> *M xoxo*

Mike was quick to respond:

> *Mare*
>
> *Italian's new, thanks for the chance to try it.*
>
> *Take your presentation outline and do the speech that goes with it. Just this time, you are writing it down, not saying it out loud. If you want to be calm and collected by the time you get to the podium, then you need to plan everything in advance. The structure is there; now you need the actual words.*
>
> *The movie was to show you how stories engage audiences; you gave it your full attention. I was looking.*
>
> *You are speaking for 25 mins, so you want to end up with about 2,300 to 2,500 words. Look at the bottom bar in Word, and you'll see the word count. Just write as if you were speaking; no need to follow the rules. Because you have the outline, writing the script shouldn't take you more than a couple of hours. Call me if you get stuck.*
>
> *M x*

Mary took a deep breath and started. She was fairly good at allowing herself to be distracted at every moment, but then 5 p.m. arrived, and she decided to finish before she left. At 7 p.m. she left the office sending Mike a text:

> *Phew. Done. Hot bath and a glass.*

Refining

Letting It Shine

Those great extroverts seem to just pop up on stage and speak fluently, without any preparation. We can do that too, right? Wrong. Let's take another little diversion.

Before turning to presentation coaching, I ran a creativity company and coached communicators to expand their creativity. I established the route that most creative people take to come up with new ideas. As part of refining the description of this process so that anyone could use it, I tested my theory on a few designers I hold in high regard. Most of them denied that they had a process; they just came up with ideas there and then. However, in observing them at work, I could clearly see that they did have a process, but it was a process that happened so quickly they were unaware of even going through it.

When we learn to drive (bear with me here), we go through Maslov's levels of competency. We start off as unconscious incompetent (what's a car?), become conscious competent (that's a car, and I can't drive it), then conscious competent (that's a car, and I've learned to drive), and finally end up unconscious competent (where shall we go for lunch?). I tried to teach my daughter to drive (one of the scariest things I have ever done) and had to remember how I drove a car because for several decades I had not had to think about it at all. As a result, I was driving terribly. Once we are competent as experienced presenters are, we can do things without apparently needing to think about them at all.

Diversion over. Those extrovert presenters we see and admire do prepare for each and every speech they make. But the preparation can take seconds because they've spent their entire lives in preparation. You and I need more deliberate action.

Rehearsal. Preparation is not only cool; for us introverts it's vital.

By now you should have a clear objective and a written text that we are going to refine by rehearsal. First, read your script out loud as many times as you need. Notice the phrases that trip you up and change them; simple repetition will make you aware of the weaknesses in your text. Once you have done this several times (and "several" will vary depending on your personal aptitude), you'll know when you've done this enough when you start to get bored.

Then it's time to look at what you are doing.

Stand up, and do the same thing but this time in front of a mirror. I told you we'd do this in small steps that introverts can cope with, but for many of my clients this is the most difficult step. Therefore, you are likely to skip it, but at that point I must become a bit of a drill sargeant about it. Get up! Do it now!

Let's take a little diversion while you reel from my sudden transformation.

If you've been following my advice, you have read the script out loud several times, so all I'm now asking you to do is the same thing but standing up and looking at yourself in a mirror. For a long time I was confused as to why this step seemed to be the most traumatic. I personally find the next step more of a problem, but that's just me, so don't worry about it for now.

Then I realized the truth thanks to the insight of one of my clients: she told me that the moment she stood up and looked in the mirror she realized that on the day she would be standing up and other people would be looking at her. That was the thing she was most scared about. Delivering the text was not what concerned her; other people judging what she delivered was what worried her.

Just remember I'm taking you by the hand here and leading you through the process one only slightly scary step at a time. See how I play both good and bad cop here?

My client's solution—once we had the insight—was that before she did the mirror thing, she put on the full war paint and dressed in her best power clothing. She realized that when we do these exercises in the privacy of our own environment, we are probably at our slobby worst. I'm writing this in the kitchen because it's the warmest room in the house and dressed for comfort, not glamour. Well, you would do that too, wouldn't you?

Using whatever technique you need to make it happen, read the script in front of a mirror and watch how you look doing it. Again, whenever you see or hear something that grates, change it to improve it.

You may also find that in the course of these exercises you want to change the end statement. It's not cast in stone. If you can say it better—or shorter, which is the same thing—then do so. Your mental attitude should be that in this phase we are in the lab (so to speak), and anything is admissible so long as it improves the presentation.

With this constant repetition you start to notice things about your text. These are things that might make you want to expand or contract whole sections. So, let's take another diversion from your rehearsals.

Back to the script. You thought I'd forgotten about that? All this repetition and constant improvement should now have produced something that is a quantum level above your first draft. It will be something that engages personally, something you now know by heart, and something to which an audience can connect—and you don't mind them doing that.

Keep up the repetition.

MARY EMBRACES PANIC: IT'S OK TO BE NERVOUS

When Mary arrived at work the next day, she found an e-mail hiding among the early morning spam. It was from her boss.

> Mary
>
> *Don't forget to include references to the company history, recent business wins, and future potential for mergers. It's important to name our influential business partners. Can you send your slides over ASAP?*
>
> George

She panicked and called Mike, who told her not to worry. "I'll have to rewrite it, and I need to do the slides this morning," she wailed. Mike advised her to spend one hour working on the things she was supposed to be doing. Don't do this now; call me when you have done all your other immediate and urgent work for the morning, and then get a coffee and call me again.

She called back 90 minutes later. Mike was in a meeting, and he returned her call at 11:30.

"Mike, I've been working on the new presentation slides for quite a while, but it's all so boring. I'm starting to panic again. What do I do now?"

"Well, to start with, stop working on the slides. Let's go back to the outline."

"But... but..."

"Outline. Mary, you are a long way down the road with this presentation, and just like with a journey, if you have to include some extra stops, it would be foolish to drive back to the start point before planning a new route. Now, first question: why is George trying to control you like this?"

"Well, um, he's my boss, so it is his job to control me."

"OK. So, do the things he's asking for actually fit into your outline?"

"Well, I've kind of covered the history, I didn't want to over-promise on the future, and the current business partners are in there but not named."

"Have you told George about your presentation?"

"No, but why can't I just make the slides and keep him happy?"

"We are nearly at the slide-making stage, but how about this: reply to George telling him how you've already included some of what he's asked for. You are going to tweak the presentation, and when you are ready, you will present to him, and he can see if there's any need for further feedback."

"God, I couldn't present to him!"

"I've got bad news for you, Mary; you are going to give this presentation in front of more than 500 people, and I'm going to suggest you rehearse it several times before then, and I think it will do you good to run through it in front of George; plus, he's your boss. He deserves to see it and have the opportunity to comment."

"Shit."

"Well, yes, but don't allow this to derail you from the process because…"

"Process? There's a process?"

"Well, yes, I was kind of leading you through it, but there is a process, and if you trust the process, I can assure you it will all turn out fine. Now just fob George off for a while and get back on track."

"But he wants slides."

"He wants to know he will *get* slides. And he will. But some people use the word *slides* when they mean *speech*, and the speech is mostly about you, not about the slides. So, tell him you'll give him the speech when it's ready for his comments."

"But he wants slides."

"Just try it. See what happens. What's the worst that can happen? I've got to go. Sorry, call me later if he comes back for more."

> *Mike*
>
> *See below*
>
> *M x*
>
> *Thursday 12:56*
>
> *Mary, sounds like you're on top of it. Ready when you are.*

George

Thursday 11.42

Dear George

I'm working through the presentation and will have my slides ready in a few days. I'd be glad if you could hear the whole thing and give me your feedback at that time.

KR

Mary

So, Mary went back to the document she'd been working on with Mike and persevered. She kept doodling her ideas for slides in the margin as she thought they would be useful. Surely Mike doesn't know everything?

Long into the evening she worked.

At 8:15 there was a knock on her office door.

It was Mike with sandwiches and a bottle of wine.

"How did you…?"

"The light was on. I can see you from across the street."

"Are you…?"

"Stalking you?"

"Are you?"

"Well…sort of. I was visiting friends who live across the street and…"

"Rich friends!"

"Is your script ready?"

"Well…"

"Show me; you've got to show someone."

And so Mary opened the wine and showed Mike the pages she'd written so far. He glanced at them and put them back on her desk.

"I'm not going to read it."

"What?"

"I want you to read it to me."

"Bugger off."

But eventually Mike prevailed. Mary read the text. And when she read, she found the things she thought would work didn't, and some of the things she thought would not work did. Every time she read it Mike suggested things to change. Every time she read it her words sounded better, but Mary was unsure whether it was the improvement in the text or the level of the bottle making the improvements.

Just before 11 they left. As they parted, Mary kissed Mike goodbye, for the first time.

"I wouldn't have got this far without you."

"Still a way to go, " he replied. "Talk tomorrow?"

They both went slowly home. Mary didn't sleep a wink.

Presenting Tips

Good to Great

Now it's time to apply those tricks of the trade, in other words, things that ramp up your presentation still further. Incidentally, all those other books written by extroverts—for extroverts—start here. This is about stage techniques that we introverts can apply only after we've done the solid foundation work of the previous steps in the process. Let's take the actions in the sequence they will happen on the big day.

To start, in all likelihood you will be introduced at the beginning of your presentation. If you do nothing about this, the chairperson of the meeting will probably read your profile in the meeting program, or worse they will make something up. Don't let this happen. We can all be described in many ways, and what matters to you now is that aspect of your character that supports your end "What do I want them to do?" statement. Construct an introduction that supports that statement to make yourself the person who is able and credible in asking for that action.

I was working with Microsoft a few years ago and saw a presentation by a company trying to sell IT to the U.K. police force. I heard an interesting grading system that I was told most police forces use. It's called *five by five* (Figure 7-1), and this knowledge changed how I look at the world—so much so that I rushed the stage to learn more!

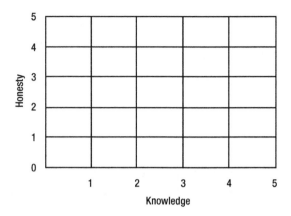

Figure 7-1. Five by five grading system

Five by five judges information on two axes, each on a scale of—you guessed it—zero to five. On one axis is the known trustworthiness of the informant, from zero (known liar) to five (always accurate in the past). The opposite axis measures the amount of knowledge the informant might have about the information, from zero (not a clue) to five (expert in the field).

So, if you thought I was trustworthy and asked me about presenting, I might be a 5/5; if you asked me about Sumo wrestling, I'd be a 5/0; and if you asked a known burglar about housebreaking, he would be a 0/5.

The purpose of your introduction is to position yourself as a trustworthy expert in the field of your chosen "What do I want them to do?" action. Only one paragraph is needed, preferably three sentences. Because these are words for someone else to say it allows you to position yourself clearly with the added value that the words will come from a third party.

If you've ever been the chair of a meeting, you'll know how relieved you'd be if the speaker simply passed you a card with the exact words nicely printed on it. Make it easy for them, and they'll not only thank you because remarkably few speakers take this step, but they'll also position you in the best way for your purpose.

So, you've been introduced, and you take the stage. The audience is ready to hear what you have to say because you have been introduced properly. And now you must begin.

We introverts don't like to think about this too much because it's the part that scares us the most. As a result, we put it out of our minds, and in the words of yet another bland business cliché, we prepare to fail by failing to prepare.

The first words you say have to be provocative.

The audience, even if you have prepared well, are sitting with their arms mentally folded—or actually folded—waiting for your pearls of wisdom and thinking "What's in it for me?" At this point you have just one sentence in which to persuade them not to update their Facebook status. I have read an awful lot of presentation books, and the "What's in it for me?" words appear in absolutely every one of them. So, among a wide variety of experts with a wide variety of attitudes and techniques, this is the common message. Therefore, your opening provocative statement needs to be personal to the audience and to hint at the final action you are going to ask.

For example, "I'd like to tell you how to be able to spend more time on your next vacation" and "All the information you have about your retirement is wrong, and I'm going to fix that" and "This new product is not just going to change your work, it's going to change your life" are all opening statements that make your audience sit up and mentally say, "That's interesting; tell me how," which is exactly the reaction you are looking for.

Let's review: you have an introduction, you have an opening provocative statement, and you have a concluding call to action. You're all set for the next chapter. See you there.

MARY STARTS ALL OVER AGAIN AND STOPS: CONSTANT REVIEW

The next morning there was this e-mail:

Mare

Look at your closing lines. Are you happy with them?

M

M

After all this you want me to change them?

No, I'm very happy, thank you very much.

I'm not changing this ANYMORE. Meetings all morning....

> *Mary*

Then that's good. Now, look at your opening and make it as provocative as you can.

At the moment it's a bit polite. Look at the close, and see if you can pose the question that answers. Call me. M

Mary was quite glad to avoid her presentation; she had a department meeting and a project meeting, and she was gulping coffee and downing painkillers. She felt dreadful. Where was the exhilaration of yesterday evening? When lunchtime came around, she "borrowed" one of the executive offices and turned the chair away from the door, put her feet up, and fell asleep. She was woken by her phone vibrating; it was Mike. She ignored the call.

She spent all day ignoring Mike's calls.

Later that night, he texted her:

> *Did you find anything at home?*
>
> Yes, about that.
>
> *What?*
>
> I'm feeling a bit pursued.
>
> *Sorry?*
>
> Just back off! How did you get my home address?
>
> *It easy to find stuff online. What's wrong?*
>
> I HATE CUT FLOWERS.

She turned her phone off. Five hours later she woke with mascara on the pillow. Dropping her clothes on the floor, she wiped her face quickly with makeup remover, crawled into bed, and turned the pillow over. Hugging herself under the covers she was asleep again in minutes.

How to Love Technology

Adding Support

Now we come to the slides. A lot of people are surprised that slides wait until this far into the process. There's a reason for this. Among event industry professionals, slides are called *speaker support,* and although that usually means slides, it can mean props, sound effects, video clips, and anything else that isn't a person at the podium talking.

The reason for the title is that slides *support* the presentation. They are not the presentation any more than the menu is the meal or the map is the territory.

I have a few things to say about slides.

A lot of people talk about "death by PowerPoint" as though it were an evil thing. It's not. Of the many types of slide preparation software out there, PowerPoint is by far the most common. It's a great program with lots of features and can produce slides of breathtaking creativity that make a great impact. However, most users only scratch the surface of what slide software can do. Slide software can execute only what you choose to put onscreen, and with that in mind, there are a few things to consider before you start making slides.

I heard Oscar-winning screenwriter William Goldman tell a group of scriptwriters how he works on a movie adapted from a book: he reads the book several times, each time using a different-colored pencil to underline key phrases. When he's finished eight or nine reads, he has a color-coded synopsis. Those parts of the book with the most underlining get into the movie, reducing as indicated until the parts that have only one or two marks might not make the final cut. Check out Goldman's excellent books on a writer's life in Hollywood, if that's of interest.

Read your now immaculate script and use a highlighter to mark the key words. Do this several times—reading out loud if possible—until you have the key words; these are the ones that really encapsulate the main points of your presentations. These are the ones that cannot be reduced further and the ones that support the progression of ideas that lead inevitably to your final call to action.

A picture does indeed say a thousand words. Your slides should have as many pictures as possible and as few words as possible.

I'll bet the room you will speak in will have lighting on the podium and little or no illumination on your audience. If you put up a slide that contains the words you are about to read, two things happen. First, your audience will read the words more quickly than you say them because we read about five times the speed at which we speak. So, your audience will have a lag between their hearing and their reading, which creates confusion. Second, the last time someone turned out the lights and read to you was probably one of your parents trying to get you to go to sleep, so your audience will hardly find this energizing. It's little wonder people fall asleep at conferences.

Your aim should be to produce the smallest possible number of slides with the fewest possible words on them, and those slides should only support your final call to action. Anything else just gets in the way. After Dinner Speaking supremo Graham Davies once told me he approaches large audiences as though they were both stupid and lazy. Individually they may be the brightest stars on the planet, but collectively they are stupid and lazy, and the greater in number, the more stupid and lazy they become. Your slides should pass the stupid and lazy test: will a stupid and lazy person get what you are going on about?

Finally, create the slides you have chosen. Your presentation will make complete sense without *any* of them. Your technology requirements will be simple and unlikely to go wrong, but if anything should happen to your slides, it will not matter.

There are loads of great freelance slide designers, and when your requirements are clear and simple, they will do a good job if you need them. If you are in the senior management of a company, it makes no sense to create the slides yourself when a professional will do a better job in much less time.

A few months ago I was asked to evaluate a startup company offering and most importantly why the company had failed to attract funding. My contact was the company chairman, who sent me the slides used in the presentation as background material. I've always believed that if you can get the full idea from just the slides, then there is no point in the speaker showing up at all.

In this case, I could see that there were two problems: an ill-thought-out business plan coupled with a poorly structured presentation because the foundations we spoke about earlier had not been well constructed. The potential investors were far from lazy or stupid, but they could not tell from the presentation why they should part with their cash. Nor was this the end point of the speech. It took very little adjustment to make the business plan more rational and to make the presentation into something that engaged with a clear direction. That's why I suggested that you avoid working on your slides until we got to this point.

Now you should have a well-constructed speech and a few well-positioned slides (if any), and you've been reading your script over and over until you are almost sick of it. You're almost ready.

MARY IS RELUCTANTLY GOING FORWARD: TRUST THE PROCESS

"Good morning, Mary. How's the presentation?"

"George! Um, I'm a bit busy this morning. How about we review it early next week?"

"I'm out next week, Mary. How about Friday morning? Say 10:30?"

"That would be, er, great!"

Mary returned to her office in a slight fog. Not only was she feeling poorly, she now had a deadline she could not miss. Three days. That meant two days to finish the slides. She took out her draft text, read it once, and headed for the coffee machine. She read it again while drinking coffee and started to scribble some slides. She looked at her schedule and realized she was already late for an internal meeting; she grabbed her coffee and her speech and rushed off.

Throughout the day Mary daydreamed through whatever she was doing, doodling on the speech as she did. By 6 p.m. she was sitting at her desk wondering what she'd done all day.

The phone rang. It was Mike.

"Mary, I'm really sorry if I upset you yesterday. I was calling to see how you're doing."

"Mary, are you still there?"

"I don't know what to say. I'm feeling a lot of pressure right now."

"Mary, I just wanted you to know I'm here if you want any help."

"Actually, I'm just starting to think about slides."

"This is the right time. What have you done so far?"

"Just doodles really. What do you do?"

"Think pictures; the slides are there to support what you're saying, not to duplicate it. The best slides are pictures with no words."

"Can I get someone else to do it for me?"

"Yes, you can, because now you are at a stage where you can brief the designer properly, but it's easy to do yourself, or you can start yourself and get a designer to tart it up later."

"I'll try on my own, and then can I send it to you?"

"Of course, Mary. I'm here if you need me."

"Thanks. I'll try some now and finish it off in the morning. Thank you."

Mary worked on for a couple of hours; once she started, things seemed to work OK. The slide software was a bit difficult, but she soon got the hang of it and liked putting in the pictures the company owned. By 8 p.m. she was exhausted but pleased. She went home and sent Mike a "thank you" text. He replied "sleep well".

Primacy and Latency

What the Audience Remembers

I mentioned earlier how stressful standing and speaking can be. If you are inexperienced, this will be even more stressful. There's a great temptation to sip a little of that free wine that's being handed around beforehand. You know, just to relax a bit.

Don't.

Your aim, remember, is to arrive at the podium calm and confident.

We've tried to make that happen by working toward the presentation by reading it out loud many times, so you know it. There's no need to actually try to remember the whole thing word for word. Actors spend years learning how to do that, and you have two advantages over them; you wrote the words, and you can have notes. I recommend having the script and reading every word.

What I suggest is that you do commit to memory your provocative opening and the final call to action. You should be able to spout either of these at any time at a moment's notice. What this means is that when you walk toward the podium, you will appear confident because you know without a moment's thought the first words you will speak. From there on, you'll find (trust me) the autopilot takes over. If you should get lost or confused at any point, you'll also be able to recover easily because your final words are also branded across the inside of your forehead in a way that's impossible to miss.

I've spent an inordinate amount of time on these first and final words because not only are they important for your own self-confidence and for the structure of your presentation, but they are also the parts of your talk that the audience is most likely to remember. If you think back to almost anything you've seen lately—TV show, movie, presentation, or stage play—if you can remember anything about them, you will recall the way they started and the way they ended. So it is with your presentation. Make sure those first and last statements really are as tight as they can possibly be.

From time to time I am asked to judge competitions or vote on awards entries for film or live events. This is interesting because it forces me to look at other people and their work. There is one glaring error of which almost all the failing entries are guilty.

When we go to see a stage play or a movie, there is a commitment; we've driven out, parked the car, arranged a babysitter, and possibly agreed to go for a meal afterward. In that situation your tolerance to a slow-starting story is very high—there's a high cost to walking out. However, in a conference with multiple streams or a DVD you watch at home, there's a much lower commitment cost.

In his excellent books on the craft of screenwriting, Jurgen Wolff gives this advice: always get into a scene at the last possible minute and get out as early as you can. The one glaring error that failing stories make is to spend too long at the start and end of each scene. We, the audience, want to get to the meat of the story as quickly as possible and then get to the conclusion of each point without great labor. This is a mistake made even by Oscar winners, so it's not unlikely that you made it too. I do, all the time.

As a final review of your presentation, ask yourself this: if I deleted the first and last quarter (keeping the opening and closing statements), would anything be lost? If not, then well done, but I have used this technique in almost every presentation I've given and found something to remove.

If you have not done so before, it's now time to give your presentation to a live person. Yep. You need to find a supportive spouse, co-worker, or friend. Stand up (this is important) and speak just as you would if you were on stage. Don't allow comments until you have finished and then ask for their honest feedback. Don't suggest things to them like "I'm unhappy with the third slide—what did you think?" Let them honestly tell you what they felt about your words.

Now, the closer your audience-of-one is to the eventual audience, the more effective they are likely to be, so if your presentation is to a bunch of 20-somethings who work in the music business, your granny might not be the person to ask. Bear in mind how distant your audience will be from your guinea pig. And remember, this is just one opinion; use the 5/5 system to evaluate each part of the feedback and so avoid slavishly following every comment—it's your presentation.

Repeat repeating the text, and subject as many people as possible to hearing it. You're almost ready for the big day.

MARY'S NEXT DISASTER: KEEP THE FAITH

Friday morning at noon Mary called Mike from the bathroom at work; she wasn't quite sobbing, but she was close. She explained how she had run through the presentation with her boss and how she felt it had gone terribly. "He just about criticized every slide," she wailed.

Mike told her that this was the point. "You want him to make those comments in privacy, not in public on the bid day," Mike reasoned. He asked her to go through all her notes and then pointed out that she had more than 2,000 words in her text. George had commented on just 12 things. She had 30 slides—Mike thought this was too many—and George had only 3 complaints. This is good news, Mike insisted.

"George just wants you to look good. And you have just faced your worst experience; this will only get better. What did he say at the end?"

"He asked me to e-mail him the revised presentation next week."

"Mary, that's great. If he'd been really critical, he would have wanted to see you perform for him again."

"What do I do now?"

"Revise, reduce, and rehearse, but first…lunch?"

"Um…."

Prepare for Performance

Stage Presence

When I first ask speakers to start by writing a script, most of them do not believe this is a way to work, nor do they believe they will be able to remember the text. After all, they are not actors. However, I hope you've found that the frequent repetition you've done means you really do know your words pretty well. The good news, of course, is that you'll have the script on the podium, so although you can remember the words, you don't need to.

It's time to prepare for the big day. The first thing is to format your script so it's easy to use and fits on the podium. I find printing in 18-point font, in landscape orientation, and on A5 paper works for me. Experiment to find what works for you. Do not bind the pages; keep them loose, which is why you *must* write the page numbers clearly on each sheet. I use a felt pen so the numbers look different from the text.

Send the slides and an electronic version of your script to the organizers. Take additional copies on a memory stick and a printout of the slides; I usually use the print option for "handouts," which shows six per page.

Make two further copies of your script printed normally to take with you. Mark the slide cues on these.

Make a small (again, I prefer A5) sheet with your introduction in 18-point type.

Now you need to run through the presentation again, in front of a person or in front of the mirror. Keep in mind that you have completed the correction and improvement stage; you are now in "show mode," so you are not going to change anything. It's done. Resist any urge you have to tinker with the text or the slides. Practice, practice, practice. Then practice some more.

Once before bed on the night before your speech, read the text one last time. It will sink in further while you sleep.

MARY'S GROWING BOREDOM: REPETITION

Over the weekend Mary repeated her presentation to the bathroom mirror, to her cat, to her roommate, and on the phone to her Mom; she even did 30 seconds to her grocer. She scribbled on her script, which she had learned to call a script, so that when she arrived in the office on Monday, she spent half an hour reworking the text and adjusting the slides. Her slides were now down to 18. She really felt she had exhausted all the possibilities. She sent the text and slides to George and got a one-line e-mail back:

Much Better. Good luck. G.

Mike's advice at this stage was simple: stop changing things. From now on, you continue rehearsing, but you've passed the revise, reduce, rehearse stage; there's only rehearse left.

Feeling brave, Mary tried the presentation out on one of her colleagues at work. He made suggestions. Mike told her to listen only to the suggestions about the way she presented; leave the content alone. Over the next week she imposed on several people at work, including someone who would actually be at the event. She had surprisingly little to say: "That'll be fine." Mary had a sudden confidence failure. "Is that all she said?" asked Mike. Mary could not recall anything else in the way she had given the presentation, nor in the reaction of her guinea pig.

Mike's advice was that some people talk only if they see something to complain about, so Mary should take the feedback as positive. Or investigate further. But he suggested that Mary didn't need any more advice; she had now practiced enough. It was time to rest and relax.

"Fat chance," Mary retorted.

As advised, Mary spent the weekend attempting to think of something else. Although she filled her time with distracting activities, her presentation was not far from her mind.

On Monday morning she was at the conference venue literally shaking with nerves, so she called Mike. He asked if she was sure the slides were correct and if she'd tried standing at the podium. He made her tell him the opening sentence and her closing line. He ended telling her that she'd done everything she could. "It's quite normal to be nervous," he reminded her. She hung up abruptly.

Standing at the podium after she was introduced, Mary felt her mouth go dry. She saw a glass of water but feared she would spill the water because her hands were shaking so much. With much trepidation, she pushed the button for her first slide and saw her name on the screen. She spoke the first sentence she had recently repeated to Mike.

And then it flowed.

The next sentence came automatically, and so did the next, and after a while she looked at her script. It was on the wrong page; she'd spoken without needing the text.

She had a moment of panic when she turned the pages to catch up. The dog-eared sheets were as familiar as anything she'd known. She turned to page 5 and lost her place. Flustered, she found it and resumed. She didn't look down once more.

Before she knew it, she was at her last slide. Her final words were looming like the end of a rollercoaster. She took a big breath and delivered the final line and heard a strange noise. She hadn't expected applause.

She rushed gratefully from the stage, sweaty, light-headed, and feeling drunk. Several people came up to speak to her, but she didn't remember what they'd said. The rest of the day passed in a blur.

Time to Shine

Let It Flow

On the big day, your objective is to walk to the podium in a confident manner. You will be nervous, but that's how it is.

Most professional actors still get nervous before every performance. Early in my theater career I was working backstage and saw that a very famous actor owned two very old enamel bowls that he placed in the wings of every theater in which he appeared. By mistake I "tided" them away; a kindly older stage manager took me to one side and explained. The bowls were there because he regularly vomited from stage fright. I heard a radio interview with the great man several years later saying that he embraced the stage fright as an important part of his performance; he said that the day he did not feel it was the day he would retire. He didn't retire.

Your objective is not to avoid feeling nervous; it is to manage it. Plan everything you can to make the experience as enjoyable as you can. When you are—naturally—nervous, you will at least know that you are well prepared, you know your speech, you are familiar with your surroundings, your message is as well prepared as it can be, and all you have to do is to say the words in the best way you can. Here's how you do that.

Arrive at the venue ridiculously early. Some try to leave as late as possible, but they miss out on a number of things. It's better to be bored than rushed. If you can possibly do so, stand at the podium and deliver some—or all—of your speech. The sound engineer will thank you, and the experience will make a big difference to your speech. If there is a slide technician, then hand over the copy of your script with the slide cues marked on it. Drink lots of water, be sure you go to the bathroom, and avoid all coffee, tea, and alcohol until afterward. You are in a delicate state—take care of yourself.

Many speakers do not like giving control of their slides to a technician, but it's really a good idea. At the least, it's one less thing to worry about, and these technicians are much better than you will be because that's all they do. When I've asked why speakers are reluctant to relinquish control of the slides, the answers I get all center on some aspect of worry about what happens if it goes wrong in the middle of the presentation. The answer to those worries is that if something does go wrong, the technician backstage is in a much better position to fix it than the sweaty nervous speaker at the podium who must keep talking at all times.

Another way of "going wrong" is that the slide might not change when you want it to, or you might go off script for some reason, and that might throw off the technician. In my experience, slide technicians are remarkably intuitive and, if you do go off script, will invariably get it right. My final thought on this is that there is absolutely nothing wrong with standing at the podium and saying "Can I have the next slide, please?" I know. Revolutionary.

While you are in the venue before the event starts, make sure your introducer has your introduction and a copy of your text if they want one; many meeting chairpeople like to know when you are likely to finish so they can prepare whatever comments they are likely to make after you have finished. Know where you will sit while waiting your turn. Actually walk the few steps from your chair to the podium. Do it several times. Make sure there is a glass of water nearby, and don't be scared to stop and drink during the presentation.

Now it's time. You are sitting comfortably, you know your material and have a numbered script ready to use as a prompt, you know the way to walk up to the podium, and your introducer has the exact words you want said. The slides are all ready, and they simply support the main points leading to your final statement. You know the first few words you will say, and you are mostly confident that once you are started, you'll be able to keep going until the end. Now you just need to say the words.

As you sit there, trying not to feel nervous but knowing it's OK that you do, I'd like to put one final thought into your head.

Think about the times you've sat in the audience and listened to a speech. What was going through your head? I'll bet you didn't have any feelings of animosity. Most audiences are actively supporting the presenter; they want to hear what you have to say or they would be in another room. They want to understand what you have to say. They want you to do well. You are not going to face the lions in the Coliseum; you are chatting to a bunch of friends. Now go and tell them the words that make you an expert.

THE END OR THE BEGINNING? POWER UNLEASHED

The next morning Mary was back in the office. It all looked the same, and no one treated her differently, but somehow it was all different. There were 15 e-mails congratulating her on the presentation she'd given the day before, and she was relieved it was over. Somehow it all felt a bit, well, flat. She looked at the detritus in her inbox; it all seemed so trivial. She hadn't expected a fanfare as she walked in, but this felt so anticlimactic.

She'd arrived home the previous evening at 7 p.m., watched TV, fell asleep on the sofa, roused herself at 9, and moved to bed; she woke ravenous at 6 a.m., ate the biggest breakfast her depleted kitchen could offer, and arrived at work good and early full of good intentions, but now she had no energy for anything.

Mike had sent a text asking how it had gone the previous afternoon, and she'd replied that she was glad it was over. That was it.

After pretending to shuffle papers around her desk and drinking too much coffee, she was woken from her fog by an e-mail from George saying that his boss had seen her presentation and congratulated George on the performance by one of the stars in his department. From the content of the e-mail Mary suspected he'd mixed her up with someone from another department.

Then Mike called to suggest a "celebratory lunch," and although she didn't feel much like celebrating, it was something to put on her empty calendar. Changing his name to suggest he might be a client, she renewed her makeup and left the office, still feeling as though she was in rehab.

He greeted her in the restaurant with a restrained peck on the cheek.

"How does it feel to have a new career?" Mike asked.

"What do you mean?"

"Things will never be the same again."

He smiled, and she broke her rule of never drinking at lunchtime.

The Aftermath

No One Asked for This

It's all over, it went better than you hoped, and there's a list of 20 things you'd do better next time. You are offered a drink and accept gratefully; several people want to talk to you. You need a strategy for handling all this.

First, about those things that didn't go the way you wanted: file them away and shut up about them. No one wants to know about that, and most of them are only in your head.

Second, you need to deal quickly with all those clamoring for your attention. This is the bit the extroverts love, but we introverts find it a bit of a challenge. My personal strategy is to have a pile of business cards for a quick swap and then to announce which part of the venue I will be in after the event. This means I'm not in a post-speech fluster and can form genuine contact with potential business partners. Channel your inner politician and glad hand as many as you can while trying to form short but meaningful contact.

Third, get out. Go to the bathroom, walk around the block, or do something that removes you from the throng. You will be so relieved the speech is over that you need some quiet time.

Fourth, reengage. Reenter the fray and see who wants some of your time.

If your presentation was captured on video, take a look at it a few days later. File away any notes for next time because there will be a next time. You have proven you can do it now. You will be asked again.

If you have slavishly followed the process I've laid out in this book, you will be a competent presenter with clarity and purpose. If this took you two weeks, then the next time it will take you three days, and the next time even less. But never lose sight of the process; however quick you get at it, always do it in the right sequence.

Most events have some form of feedback mechanism used, and this can be informative, but it's also dangerous stuff. You'll want to evaluate it differently in different situations. For example, you can use the feedback very specifically if you are likely to give the same presentation again at a different time, and you'll also want to see where you can improve overall in the way you construct your appearances. Generally, I find that the feedback you have yourself—the feeling you have as you leave the stage—is a much harsher critic than anyone in the audience. There is also the issue of what questions were asked in the feedback. Look at this very critically.

Management consultants are fond of two-by-two grids, so here is one:

	Done Right	Done Wrong
Doing the Right Thing	Right Thing Right	Right Thing Wrong
	Wrong Thing Right	Wrong Thing Wrong

Doing Things Right

This is a bit confusing until it's explained. The grid is comparing whether something is done badly or well. Doing Things Right appears along the bottom axis, so on the left are things done well (Done Right), and on the right they are things done badly (Done Wrong). On the vertical axis, we are comparing whether we are doing the correct thing (Doing the Right Thing) or the wrong thing.

Some examples might be that if you were hosting a dinner party, you might be a good cook and therefore able to Do Things Well, but if I was a vegetarian and you cooked meat, it does not matter how well you cooked it; it would not be a meal I would like to eat. So, you'd be doing the wrong thing and doing it very well.

You may think this is a bit pedantic and deliberately using confusing words. However, it's making what is in my mind an important point, and it's one that produces some very muddled thinking particularly in the interpretation of event feedback.

Event organizers are often guilty of focusing on the wrong thing and of taking great care to get the wrong thing very right indeed. From the dinner party example, I hope you can see that it better to do the right thing badly than it is to do the wrong thing very well. If I were vegetarian, I would be happier with poorly cooked food I can eat than with excellently prepared stuff that I can only look at.

Feedback is also an excellent way of improving on the wrong thing and doing it better and better over the years. Meaning, the vegetarian is delivered ever better steak.

It's important this distinction is not lost, not misinterpreted, and not used to make your presentation less than the fantastic speaking opportunity you made into the best piece of communication it could possibly be.

Now that you are an experienced presenter, you can use the skills you have learned here in many aspects of your working and personal life. We introverts will never be entirely comfortable in the spotlight, but with planning and care we can learn to enjoy it and become very good at it, while managing the process and continuously improving.

The Last-Minute Panic

Emergency Preparation

It's 9 p.m., and you've arrived at the hotel. The conference starts tomorrow at 8:30 in the morning. You have a note from the event producer asking you to visit the conference room at 7 a.m. Up to now you've been too busy to give your presentation a moment's thought. Now there's a sick feeling in your stomach, and the mini bar looks inviting.

I was once called to a client conference on rehearsal day and asked to offer tips to the speakers. There was one woman I could not help much. She was very elegant, she had a great speaking manner, and her assistant had briefed a great designer to produce about 30 slides covering every aspect of her department. She ended her rehearsal slot by flicking through the remaining ten slides and muttering, "I'll think of something to say at the end." Up to that point I'd been impressed at her ability to make a decent effort with material she had clearly only just seen.

I took her to one side and offered my assistance. Her reply: "I have only 20 minutes to get ready for the welcome dinner. There's no more that can be done." With that she swept out of the room, four assistants following with notepads. The following day she was better than rehearsal but still not prepared. She lasted five more months with the company.

I'm not saying this to frighten you. You're scared enough already. I am saying it to make you focus on those things you can do—right now—to improve your chances on stage tomorrow. Follow me and you *will* be OK.

Yes, you should have done it earlier. Yes, it won't be perfect. Yes, you can beat yourself up…but we can do all we can. This involves not putting it off anymore, and you have no time to waste, so let's get on with it.

First, call room service. No one does well in a stressful situation on an empty stomach.

Now, while the food is on its way, it's time to really, really focus. So, get a sheet of paper and write down the *one* thing you want your audience to know when you have finished speaking.

There was—allegedly—a poster on the wall in Bill Clinton's campaign office that said this: "If you say more than one thing, you have not said anything at all." In today's crowded environment an audience wants a compelling message it can understand and act on. Get really clear about the *one* thing you want to say.

Another way to look at it is to think "If I could say only one thing, what would it be?"

You need to achieve a Zen-like calm about this important message; let the million thoughts flooding your head clear away and decide on this one message. Your success on stage tomorrow depends on this one thought. It's tempting to allow all the many things you could say cloud your judgment, but if you can achieve this clarity, it will do wonders for the success of your presentation.

Still with me? OK, you have one thing written down. Pin it up somewhere you can see it; the room is going to get messy.

Now you can have supporting facts. And these will get confused in your mind because your mind will now try to shoehorn in all the facts you have and confuse the issue. So, write down all the things you can think of, each one on a separate piece of paper. Sticky notes work well if you have some. I find those little pads of hotel notepaper useful too.

The more expert you are, the more of these you will have, and I know you're an expert. How do I know that? You've been invited to speak, of course, and you know so much about your topic you have not bothered to prepare.

Using your great expertise, generate loads of facts that support your main message. Go on. You've been told since the age of five not to make a mess, and here I am positively encouraging you. Anyway, no one can see. Except me. I am everywhere.

Do that and join me back here when you're done.

Now the tricky bit. Actually, the only tricky bit.

You have to choose just three of those facts to support your main message. This is where Darwinism comes in. It's survival of the fittest. Allow your facts to engage in gladiatorial combat until only the strongest survive. It will be a bloody fight, but you will have those three that emerge victorious.

Now, it's time to tidy up. Write your main message and your three supporting facts here.

Main Message

Supporting Fact 1

Supporting Fact 2

Supporting Fact 3

You now have your content. No more is required. The tricky stuff is over; it's all process from here on out.

Next, make a story. How do these three facts tell the main message you have? This is the bit we all know how to do, although sometimes we pretend we don't. To engage the most useful part of your brain, imagine that you meet an old friend for a drink. This friend knows nothing about your chosen career, and casually he asks: "What do you mean by that?"

Pay close attention to your answer.

One mistake often made in presentations is that we forget how to speak, reverting to industry jargon and trying to speak like a lawyer or like a piece of written prose. This is a speech. Speak like a human, and your audience will understand you.

Now it's time to write your actual words.

Twenty minutes is 1,200 seconds. Humans speak about three words for every two seconds. So, a 20-minute talk needs about 800 words. It's about the number of words in this chapter up to here.

If you are speaking for more than 20 minutes, then don't use all the time. No one wants to hear more. No audience member will complain if the coffee break comes early; no conference organizer will complain if you are the one to get things back on track after earlier speakers ran long. The worst thing that will happen is that you get time to take questions.

At this point, if you have time, I highly recommend writing out your speech in full, but I know you are keen to put this behind you, so you might be tempted to just list topic headings on some 3x5 cards or scamp out the presentation as a mind map. Frankly, it's whatever floats your boat. Get the thing in a format that is as clear for you as it can be.

Read it through out loud a couple of times and see how long it takes.

Adjust accordingly.

Now it's time to look at slides. At a minimum, you may use five slides.

- Your name and the title of your talk
- Point 1
- Point 2
- Point 3
- Your key message

Anything more is just showing off.

Author and Apple evangelist Guy Kawasaki has a rule for presentations that he calls 10/20/30:

- No more than ten slides
- Speak for no more than 20 minutes
- Use 30-point type or larger

Whenever you can use a picture instead of words, your slides will have more impact. We remember pictures; we do not remember text. Remember, use as few slides as possible and as many pictures as possible. Show, don't tell.

If you already have a prepared slide deck, you may like to use a little-known function of your slide program: the Delete button. Ruthlessly cut out any slides that do not help your story.

Now you have a story to tell, and you have a nice, memorable terse set of slides to help you tell that story.

It's time to rehearse again, with slides this time, and then go to bed. You need your sleep, and the presentation will—magically—embed itself while you sleep. Plus, tomorrow is your big day.

Nerves will affect you; nerves are just excitement with bad PR. By keeping your message simple, keeping your objective clear, and removing distracting slides, you have minimized this. By keeping the presentation concise and focused, there is less time to worry.

There are a few additional things that will help you get through the day.

- Have a good breakfast.
- Don't drink coffee.
- Keep a bottle (not a glass) of water with you at the podium.
- Remember those in the audience want you to succeed.
- Get to the room early and rehearse on stage as much as possible.
- Above all, remember where you are going.

While I have you, you might think "that went OK," and it will go OK. But if you want to really wow your audience, this is simply not good enough. The great orators are great because they spend time getting the presentation just perfect. Winston Churchill estimated that each minute of a speech takes one hour of preparation, which means three working *days* of preparation for one twenty-minute speech.

Using the steps I've described here, you'll be fine. You could be exceptional.

Case Study

JCN Software

Step 1: Preparation

I waited in the boardroom for Barry. I was given the nice cups and posh snacks, which were all indications of status, as was his keeping me waiting for 15 minutes. He walked in talking on his phone and waved to me, pouring himself coffee while carrying on the conversation.

"Did you get my presentation?"

I replied that I had received his slides: all 35 of them for a 20-minute presentation.

Barry pulled out his laptop. I put my hand on it to stop him and told him I'd like to talk about the context first.

If I'd grabbed his crotch, the body language could not have been more dramatic. He put the laptop down but not away. As he spoke, he absentmindedly wiped the place I'd touched the laptop with his sleeve.

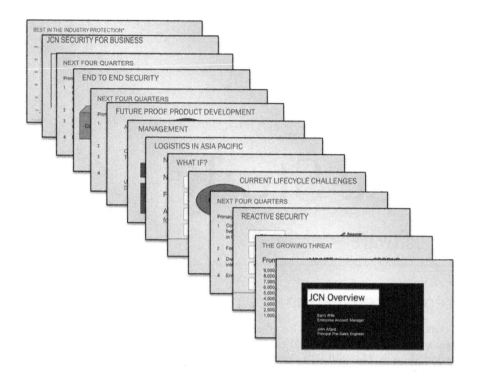

"My assistant has been working on those slides for over a week," he said while taking out a printed version of the same thing. He clutched it to his chest like some kind of security blanket.

In my coaching work I'm a bit of a development magpie, picking up bits and pieces from any number of techniques, philosophies, psychological models, and influencing skills.

The thing I use most of all is simple: observing body language and then seeing how it changes with each piece of added input from me. With practice, it gets to be easy to identify the anxieties that need to be overcome.

Barry was scared. Barry was also unable to tell me what he was scared about. The reliance on slides is a frequent symptom; my first job was to get him to talk about something else.

Barry's boss had suggested he work with me. Recently promoted to management, Barry knew the technical side of his business well. His business was software security. The promotion meant Barry was now required to give presentations regularly; this opportunity was his baptism by fire. I also suspect Barry's boss was afraid his new recruit might prove an embarrassment.

I told Barry I had seen the slides and had looked over them the night before. I also took out a notepad and began to write.

I rarely need to refer to any notes I take in a coaching session, but some people—and I guessed Barry was one of them—take comfort from the knowledge that facts are being recorded. In fact, at the end of my process, it matters not a bit whether I remember the facts of the presentation; it only matters whether Barry remembers. No one I have coached has ever taken notes.

Small steps were needed with Barry. I started by asking questions I could not know from looking at the slides; I asked about the audience, the time of day, the venue, and the other speakers. It was all interesting stuff for me, but the real purpose was to get Barry thinking about the context in which his presentation would be received.

As any event producer will tell you, context is everything. I remember as a child watching *Monty Python* on the BBC. The program was scheduled just before the evening news, which then on at 9 p.m. I recall laughing through the first few items of the news; that's how powerful the *Monty Python* sense of the absurd was. It took a really shocking opening news story to break the spell.

Barry told me that his company mostly sold to other IT companies, and the event at which he was speaking was the annual gathering for people in the Internet security business. So, the audience would be a gathering of his peers, competitors, and potential customers.

Although I had looked at the slides, they had been so dense with jargon and mysterious diagrams that I had not really understood them. That's quite common; I am not in the Venn diagram of his audience.

A little more probing established that Barry's main concerns were to get across the details of his company's new product, impress his peers, and begin the sales process with those people in the audience who might be prospects.

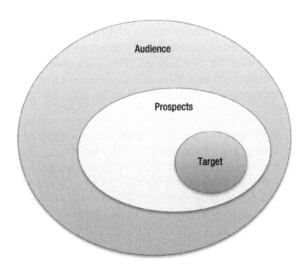

It's common that a presentation is actually aimed at a small percentage of the audience. I have known presentations made in an auditorium seating more than 1,000 where the actual message was for just one person. It's not as mad as it sounds. Sometimes that's the only way to get that one person to listen to you. Sometimes you need the peer pressure of an ovation to convince. Sometimes there's one decision maker and a whole load of other people who could say "no," and then there's the prestige of being a speaker that adds to the credibility of the message.

I suggested to Barry that we focus on his prospects and then address any potential fallout, if there was any, in the other groups later. This was a mistake on my part because it allowed him to pick up his precious slides again. I learned just how desperately he was clinging to the life raft of the slides his assistant has created.

"I don't have time to rework any of these," he claimed.

Of course, the words "I don't have time" are always a front for something else; sometimes it means "other things are more important" or "I'm not prepared to give my attention to this," but my feeling was that Barry was still in what I call procrastination mode. He was putting off his preparation until it was simply too late. It was time for me to change tack.

I asked him what he wanted from our time together. The truth that I knew, but he did not know that I knew, was that his boss had been coached by me a few months before and had decided that this presentation was simply too important to be left to chance. Barry had been told to use me. This is never a good way to start a coaching session. The coachee often responds like a truculent teenager, and it's difficult to make progress without adopting a poor impression of a remedial teacher.

All things considered, Barry was being more adult in his attitude than he might have been, but the anxiety needed to be removed. So, I tried changing the subject; I told him we needed to discuss the exact message he was using with his slides (suggesting that he didn't need to change them although that was my aim), but first I'd like to take a look at his personal style. I asked him about presentations he admired and then on to films he liked, TV shows he enjoyed, and books he read.

It's surprisingly easy to get the people I coach off the topic of their presentation, particularly if they are procrastinators. As you'll see, this is not just my wasting time with a nice chat; I was also trying to get Barry away from the blind panic of clutching to his slides as though they were his presentation. The scariest thing I could have said to Barry was that the audience is not coming to see his slides; they are coming to see *him*.

The background also gives me insight into the kind of story Barry was best at telling. It's all a bit of neurolinguistic programming (NLP), but I watch him like a hawk as he tells me things with his words and mostly with his body.

Having dragged his attention away from the slides, I told Barry I didn't fully understand his business or its products, so I asked him to explain in layperson's terms what the point was of the new product.

It's true that I didn't really understand any of the intricacies of cloud-based IT security in the finance sector, but my ignorance was not the reason for the question. I wanted to see whether Barry could speak like a human and not use the language on his slides that were clearly written by Spock.

I'd already persuaded him to talk about something other than his presentation, and he seemed to be an intelligent human being. Now I was bringing him back to the topic but from another angle. It worked for a while, and he explained the new product in ways that made sense to me as someone who wanted to be able to do my banking and shopping online. Then he reached for his slide printout, and the techspeak came back. There was one big difference, however; this time he didn't clutch his slides like a security blanket but spread them messily across the table and was pointing to the relevant images and underlining them with a pencil.

Progress. Now I knew he would be able to change his slides; all I needed was for him to know that too.

Barry then bought up the often-asked question of where to stand. He started with the assumption that his laptop would be on the podium, and he would stand behind it. But he'd seen a TED Talk, and that speaker didn't have anything on stage; she just walked around. Barry liked this look and wanted to emulate it. He was worried about how he could operate his slides and whether he could pull it off.

We talked a little about Barry's anxieties before I was able to tell him a few things about staging.

- If everyone else is using the podium, then it's a way to stand out.

- There are lots of ways to cue slides without being near your laptop.

- If the podium is there, you can always retreat behind it.

- Once you've moved away from the podium, you are unlikely to return.

I wanted Barry to feel able to experiment, so we planned to try a few different options during rehearsal. That seemed to calm him, and we moved on to other things.

Step 2: Objective

The next move was to make my "magic question." This is a technique I have stolen from the work of Mark McKergow and Solutions Focus. I said I was a magpie.

I asked Barry what would happen if everything went wrong on the day and he could show just one slide.

The sequence I use in coaching differs depending on the person I'm working with. I sensed Barry was ready to consider the possibility that the order of the slides might alter, but as I was still asking him to help me understand his message, I wasn't actually saying this out loud. I was also using this as a roundabout way to get to his ultimate objective.

The magic question often produces lengthy agonizing, but in Barry's case he was surprisingly decisive, selecting a slide that was number 23 out of 35.

I then asked him why that was the pivotal slide.

"It shows our changes to the architecture that improve usability for the user while increasing security for the finance house and the merchant. It's really the only thing we've done that is truly revolutionary."

Quite often I can tell when I'm coaching experts in their field. They have too many slides because they know too much. The problem isn't understanding; it's understanding what matters.

If I were being cruel at this point, I'd ask Barry why he needed the other 34 slides, but I thought he was still a little fragile for that kind of challenge.

I tried to understand the implications of the new product by Socratic inquiry. Basically this means acting like my daughter when she was three and just asking "Why?" after every answer until the plain truth becomes obvious. Even to me.

I then asked Barry to find three slides that contained hard facts—facts that supported the message given on slide 23. This proved more difficult, and he initially circled eight slides on his printout.

I eliminated those that were not hard facts—facts that could not be disputed by anyone in the room. Now we were down to four. I asked him to rank them in terms of importance to the key slide and simply suggested he take the top three. This produced the most agony to date.

It was time for a refill of coffee to break the tension. I even managed one of the nice snacks.

Having established the three supporting slides, I told Barry it didn't matter if it was three, two, or four, but there needed to be a small number of facts that the audience could take away.

I don't think he noticed the switch from talking about my understanding to talking about the audience. That subtle shift allows me to overtly suggest that his slide deck might be reordered. One of the three supporting slides appeared *after* slide 23.

Time for magic question 2.

I asked Barry to focus on the prospects in the audience. What would be the best outcome after his presentation?

"I want them to place an order and credit me with the sale."

We talked about that for a while. It wasn't likely that anyone in the audience would actually have an order pad with them nor the authority to place an order immediately. So, I pushed for a more realistic outcome.

"I want 50 percent of my target prospects to contact me, either on the day or soon after."

That was SMART in every sense.

Specific
Measurable
Achievable
Realistic
Timely

I then suggested that in order to make that happen, we might reorder his slides a little. Barry took it very well and reached for his laptop again. I stopped him once more.

I told him we had a clear objective and that we had agreed to alter the order of the slides, but I wanted to take one more step before we did that.

Step 3: Outline

In presentation coaching work, I find I spend very little time actually coaching. This next part of our session was almost all directive. Coaches move on a line between coaching (helping you find the answer you already know) to mentoring (telling you facts that allow you to make decisions on your own) to instructional (teaching you things) and finally directives (telling you what to do). The skill—it seems to me—lies in knowing where you are and where you should be at all times.

There was a flip chart in the room; I asked Barry to write his desired outcome at the bottom of the sheet.

Above that I told him to leave a space.

Above that he summarized his key slide.

Above that he wrote the three supporting facts; then I allowed him one more.

Opener
Supporting Fact 1
Supporting Fact 2
Supporting Fact 3
Outcome

Above that I told him to write "Opener."

There's no "right" way to do it, but this seemed the best way given Barry's state of nervousness and the way he'd prepared for our meeting.

What I was hoping was to find the story Barry could tell. I was then hoping he would either completely rewrite his slides or radically edit them. But first things first: we needed a structure.

What Barry had written on the flip chart was the basics of a structure lacking two key elements. First I wanted to address his closing sentence.

He had the objective clear; he wanted 50 percent of the prospects in the audience to contact him after he'd spoken. I asked Barry to come up with a call to action that might achieve that.

"What about an incentive?" he asked. "I could offer them something to get in touch for."

We talked about a qualifier. It's easy to get a response for a freebie, but that would appeal to everyone in the room; we wanted just the prospects to respond. So, we needed to find an incentive that would appeal only to those in the market for his company's product and with the budget and authority to act.

Barry suggested he would talk to his boss about this, which relieved me.

In coaching we often get hung up on one particular detail while losing sight of the bigger picture. I was keen that Barry found what he was looking for, but in this instance I didn't mind what that was. I really wanted to get back to his presentation.

I then asked Barry to think about his opening.

"Ladies and Gentlemen, it's an honor and a pleasure to be asked to speak here today" was his suggestion.

I almost fell asleep.

I asked if there was something provocative he could say—something that would wake up his audience and really make them pay attention.

Barry felt he had to be polite, so I asked what he would say if he *didn't* need to be polite.

"We are going to take over the world, and you'll all be out of a job in three years."

Well, that would certainly get attention. Could he actually follow through and prove that? Barry told me he could, but he didn't want to be so aggressive.

Sometimes we need to be in touch with a deeper feeling in order to then pull back to the more polite version.

For now, I asked Barry to write "All out of a job" in the "Opener" space.

I asked him to step back and take a look at his *outline*.

We were nearing the end of our first session and were due to meet again in four days. I gave him homework to do. He was to write his own script. Word for word—write 1,800 words because that's all you'll have time for.

"I can't remember a script; that's not how I work," he protested.

I told him not to worry about that. He might remember the words; he might not. This exercise was about formulating the ideas and getting the outline fleshed out into something solid.

"But what about my slides?" Barry really was clutching at straws.

I told him not to worry about the slides either; his slides were lovely (they weren't, but that message was for another day). I told him just to focus on the text for now, and we'd work on the rest of his presentation the next time.

Barry wasn't sure, but he left promising to write something anyway.

Step 4: First Draft

Four hours before we were next due to meet, Barry's assistant sent me an e-mail saying he was too busy to see me. I replied, telling her I would still be charging for the cancellation.

If someone were to try to write the algorithm that dictates my charging policy, it would be very complicated, and I'm not sure I understand it myself.

By canceling/postponing on the day by e-mail and getting his assistant to do it, Barry had three strikes against him, so I showed no mercy. I also suspected this was another power play that I find repulsive, so make that four strikes.

Strangely, clients often cancel the second meeting. It's probably because they have not done their homework, but also it's because the reason they need me in the first place is because procrastination is taking hold of any preparation they should be doing. Postponing me when they are not personally paying the bill is just another form of procrastination.

We finally met three days later. I am always early for meetings, but Barry was ahead of me sitting in the boardroom with his typed text in his hand and another copy for me. Good boy.

Step 5: Refinement

"Would you like time to read it?" asked Barry, eager as a puppy.

I told him I didn't want to read it; I wanted him to read it to me, standing at the other end of the room.

That knocked him back, but for a good reason.

As Barry read his text, I deliberately did not look at my copy. I looked at him as he read. I was gauging a number of things as he read: the text, his speaking style, how familiar he was with the words, whether it made sense to the virgin ear, and how he was standing.

It seemed to me he had actually written the words himself; he had also never read the words out loud before. His presentation style was fine.

There was lots of work to do, but the basis was solid.

As soon as he finished, he scuttled back to his seat. I immediately made him get up and do it again. This time I did follow the text with my copy, marking those points where Barry diverted from the script and those passages he found difficult.

If something is not working in the message and the concept, then this is the last chance to fix that. If there are minor technicalities to get over, then I become a technician suggesting things that Barry might find easier.

We worked through the text three times before I decided enough was enough. I suggested Barry type up the reworked script and that our session was at an end. He looked worried.

"How will I remember all that?" he asked. "And when can I mark the slide cues?"

I explained that while he might or might not remember the whole thing, this was part of the process that we would look at the next time and that the slides would also be put in at the next session.

Sometimes I get to the slides during session 2, but in this case I felt Barry's attention should be on the words he was going to say.

Step 6: Final Draft

My third, and final, session with Barry arrived, and I managed to persuade him that this session should be offsite. I knew the conference center where he was due to speak and had managed to book a small room there. But that wasn't my intended venue.

As soon as Barry arrived, I asked him to walk with me, and we took a tour of the building, including the main hall where some technicians were moving staging around. Checking with them, we trespassed on the stage for a while.

I asked Barry to try speaking in the room, with no microphones, no script, no witnesses (except the technicians who could not have cared less), and no pressure.

Of course, Barry did most of his speech from memory; he mucked up a bit of it, and he missed out about half a page.

We returned to our little room with Barry's head held high.

We talked—a lot—about how Barry felt standing on the stage, including how he would feel when he was in the same place in one week's time, how the technicians were completely indifferent, and how surprised he was at how much of the script he'd remembered.

Of course, the slight mistakes he'd made passed without causing him any panic attack because it was just an empty room and did not matter. When his peers and prospects were watching him, everything would matter massively.

Step 7: Visual Support

It was time to talk slides.

Having persuaded Barry to ignore the slides, I watched his face fall when I brought it up.

I often think of my job as guiding clients on the roller coaster that is presentation preparation. Like them, I hate presenting. Like them, I am prone to procrastination. Like them, I need a kick on the backside occasionally. Unlike them, I have a robust process that I know works, and clients seem to enjoy leaving the process to me.

Slides. Barry was now worried that his newly scripted presentation did not match his slides. I told him how we would now edit the slides to match the script.

I've been accused of being a bit down on slides. I constantly tell my coaching clients *not* to focus on the slides.

That's not because they are not important; they are very important. Slides are just not where you start from in preparing a presentation; they are where you end up.

Earlier I referred to Guy Kawasaki's formula 10/20/30:

- No more than ten slides.

- Speak for no longer than 20 minutes.

- Use no smaller than 30-point type.

With all things presentation, there are no "rules." There are only guidelines. *Apply the previous formula unless there is a good reason not to.*

Guy Kawasaki's Rules	
10	Slides
20	Minutes
30	Point Type

Now that Barry had a compelling story to tell, slides are great for amplifying that message into a truly memorable piece of communication.

There is an oft-quoted piece of research that shows that if we hear information, we recall about 12 percent. If we see information, we recall slightly more, about 19 percent. But if we have congruence between what we hear *and* what we see, the figure goes up to more than 60 percent.

Like most oft-quoted research, this is utter rubbish that gets repeated often enough because the underlying principle is sort of right.

In fact, recall is incredibly variable. The defining factors are the type of information, the audience's engagement with the message, the learning styles of the audience, and the skill of both the words and the visuals used.

Another way of looking at it is that your audience will have a number of different learning styles; you need to hit all of them. For more information on this topic, take a look at any of the Accelerated Learning books available. There are links to some of them on The Introverted Presenter web site.

Slides are great for supporting what you are saying. They are rubbish at replacing your talk, and they are positively damaging if the messages on the slide conflict with your words. This happens surprisingly often.

Once you have a clear objective and text, it's time to create slides that help that message along.

Among event professionals, slides are often called *speaker support*, which is strange in that—as far as I know—it's the only professional expression that is *longer* than the layperson's term. Professional terms are usually ways for those in the profession to save time.

The reason is that slides are (once again) there to *support* your message.

That's what they are good for.

Creating slides is easy; Barry was going about it the hard way. He only really needed five slides.

> Opening proposition
>
> Supporting Fact 1
>
> Supporting Fact 2
>
> Supporting Fact 3
>
> Final conclusion or call to action

Anything else is just decoration.

Barry had his assistant design the slides. He seemed like an intelligent guy, but he was certainly no designer. There are many designers out there who spend all day every day just making slides. I know many executives who spend their night hours producing slides when someone costing one-third of their hourly rate could do a much better job. Why is this? They don't know what to say to a designer. Well, Barry could (if he were starting from scratch) now be in a position to brief a designer very concisely.

From the five slides you might want to expand, remember Guy Kawasaki's advice: use no more than ten slides unless there's a really good reason to do so.

Your slide designer (even if it's you) will do far better to produce eight lovely slides than thirty "death by PowerPoint" slides.

I find the act of describing what I need to a designer helps me to clarify my messages; the interrogation I get from a designer strengthens my message and sometimes exposes weaknesses in my story.

It also helps me with my timekeeping. When I begin to write a presentation, the first thing I do is to book a session with my favorite designer in—say—five days' time. That makes me do everything else in the following five days—well, alright, sometimes in the fourth of five days.

Here's a test of whether your slides are doing their job: can you tell the story just from the slide? If so, then you have too much information. Simplify the slides until they express only the most basic principle of your topic.

There is one exception, often quoted, to this idea. In investment presentations, particularly in the finance sector, slides are used quite differently. The rest of you: no excuses.

You've probably seen the prompting systems that are on the front of every camera in a TV studio and used by CEOs, presidents, and celebrities to deliver speeches. Well used, they are a terrific way to give a professional presentation while not needing to commit the whole thing to memory.

But that's not what slides are for.

When the presenter simply reads the slides to the audience, the slides fail for two reasons:

- The first reason is that often presentations are done in darkness, or at least subdued lighting. Our parents did a great job programming us by reading bedtime stories. Human beings are therefore often programmed by low light levels and someone reading to us; we go to sleep. Even if your audience are not actually asleep, they will certainly be drowsy.

- The second reason is that we read faster than we speak. Before you finished the first line of your slide, the audience has finished reading the whole slide and is now thinking about what to cook for dinner. You've lost them.

Either way, your slides are not supporting your message; they are detracting from it.

I explained to Barry that his slides are prompts for him. The simple statement that each slides contains will remind him of the next part of his talk; they will intrigue his audience and then build enlightenment as he explains why the abstract concept shown really supports his message. A presentation, like the telling of all good stories, will gradually unfold in the mind of your audience.

With other clients, this stage is where I sometimes help them to *create* the slides—often having a graphic designer attend the third session. However, I felt Barry was attached to his current slides and would have resisted. I had a printed copy of his slides to work on, and Barry started scribbling to reorder, edit, and delete those slides that did not now match his text.

It didn't take long.

Barry even called his assistant and dictated the changes over the phone.

At the end, he had just 15 slides for his 20-minute presentation, but I felt there was more work we could do. The crucial slide, the one you use if there's only time for one, was the final "call to action" slide.

Normally, in my opinion, if the slides tell the story, then they don't do the job. A speaker who reads his slides is at a loss from the beginning because the audience can read much faster than the speaker can speak. The one exception to this rule is the final "call to action" slide. That slide will stay onscreen as you leave the stage; it's the one thing your audience *must* remember. So, in that case, I believe in being very literal, unless there's a reason not to. Obviously.

I shared my feelings about Barry's slides, but we agreed to revisit them once his assistant had made the changes.

Step 8: Rehearsal

I then asked Barry to read through his script one more time. This time he needed to anchor those things he had done well, to get feedback, and to enhance his performance.

I was working with the experienced event producer Fran O'Linn when I heard her tell a client: "This is the rehearsal where we practice what we are going to do; it's not where we decide *what* to do. You had that chance."

Fran is an actress and strict task master; she would not allow changes after a certain point. I'm not sure I am so strict, but the point is well made.

Barry was beginning to embed his performance, to perform without thought, and further changes were likely to upset that.

We talked about Barry's script. Some presenters like to put topic headings on 3x5 cards, others like to have the script on the podium to read from, and still others like to commit everything to memory.

Barry decided to have his full script with him on the day. I gave him some techniques for successfully presenting from a script.

I didn't mention how much he'd been against this at the start.

Some unprepared presenters can show the audience the top of their head when reading a script. They talk *to* the script, which means they talk as if the audience were 18 inches away. So, there's no eye contact and a mumbling delivery.

The secret to delivering a presentation with a full script is to look down and see the next sentence and then look up and deliver that sentence to the audience. Then look down again.

As Barry had proved, he actually knew a lot of his speech, so the amount he needed to look down is quite slight. However, taking a moment of silence to look down can seem far too long to the speaker, but to the audience it's completely natural.

Barry was also worried that in his new role he might not be taken seriously. He was young for the role and would be addressing many people who were older than he was.

I suggested that his fear was only *his* concern.

Simply by standing at the podium Barry would be seen as an expert. This is one of the best reasons to cultivate a public speaking career. However, if that was not enough, I suggested Barry might like to consider delivering his speech more slowly.

Some of the most impressive speeches are made by people who speak very slowly. If you recall Martin Luther King's famous "I Have a Dream" speech, he delivers the words incredibly slowly. Winston Churchill and Nelson Mandela were also slow speakers and made all the more impact because of that.

By the time we'd worked through the rehearsal, the slides had been e-mailed back. One final run-through and a few tweaks and Barry was ready.

Well, I thought he was.

Step 9: Performance

I spoke to Barry on the phone 24 hours before he was due to give his presentation. "Can you come over now?" he asked. I explained that it wasn't really necessary—he was ready to present. But as it happened, I was coaching another presenter near the conference center where Barry was due to speak, so we met for coffee.

My job was to reassure Barry that he *did* know everything he needed to know. I asked him to give me the presentation sitting in the coffee area. Not only was he fairly word perfect, he even unconsciously twitched his finger every time a slide cue happened. We had several strange looks from the other customers in the coffee shop, none of which caused Barry to flinch. So, I'd checked my assumption that he was ready.

Barry had attended a rehearsal and had—at my suggestion—given control of the slides to the technician running the event. He really had nothing to worry about. But something in the morning had unnerved him.

I asked how the rehearsal had gone.

"Not bad. The technician was very nice and seemed surprised when I gave him a marked script. I stood on stage, but they only allowed me a soundcheck, not a full run-through. I offered to read through the speech for the technician, but he was quite dismissive. I'm not sure handing it over was the best thing."

And I had it right there; Barry had relinquished control and was feeling the lack of it.

I always recommend giving control away to the technician if at all possible, assuming there is one. These people do this every day and will be far better positioned to correct things if anything goes wrong—most mistakes in slide cueing happen because of a sweaty-fingered presenter nervously pushing buttons too often. I also believe that a laptop on the podium is yet another barrier between a presenter and the audience.

I told Barry that in this case I would normally tell him to practice some more, but his recitation was so close to the script, he need have no fear on that score.

"But I missed some bits."

Actually, he didn't leave anything out; he just paraphrased a bit. It was nothing that affected his final message, and it was nothing that the audience would notice.

When I first left home to study at drama school, I was lent an apartment by an actor while I found somewhere of my own to rent. My school friend Chris and I stayed in Balham in South London for a week before we found our first student house. In the apartment was a book called *Cooking in a Bedsitter* by Katherine Whitehorn full of valuable advice for living on your own, mostly about cooking but also a philosophy book for the newly independent. It contained this advice: remember, there is no polite answer to the question "I forgot to do the mushrooms; would you have liked some?"

In the same way, if you alter your presentation on the fly or even forget a bit, no one in the audience will be any the wiser unless you draw attention to it. So, don't.

Many years later I found myself sitting opposite Katherine Whitehorn at a restaurant and became a giggly fan attempting to express my gratitude. She was very gracious, but this clearly, unsurprisingly, happened a lot.

Barry wasn't really calmed by my words of wisdom; he really wanted to take control of the slides back. I applied a bit of NLP asking him to imagine himself on stage with the excitement of delivering his finely honed words to the expectant crowd. Excitement and stage nerves are merely different sides of the same coin.

He admitted to feeling the excitement building in him. I asked what was best about the experience. "The connection with the audience," he replied without any thought.

Fussing over stage props, slides, and everything else only gets in the way of that connection. Even if the slides go completely wrong, if the projector breaks, and if the slide technician dies backstage, you still have a story to tell that can be helped with slides but not ruined without them.

I told Barry to focus on his words, not anything else. The audience has come to hear him speak, not to watch him show some slides.

What I think I do in most of my coaching relationships is to advise my clients where to put their attention at each stage of the process. When we do anything that's unfamiliar, our brains try to grab hold of the parts we think we know about. We veer away from the unfamiliar and consequently give it as little attention as we can. The coach's job is to reverse this natural tendency.

Barry was focusing on his slides because, to him, that was the familiar tendency. Taking that away from him forced him to think about the part he really didn't want to do. By applying the thoughts of how the presentation could go, I hoped to get his neural pathways starting to focus on the important part of his performance.

We had talked—a lot—in all our sessions about the questions that would come from the floor. Barry was scared by this unplanned part of his presentation. There are quite a lot of strategies for handling questions, and I led him through the best for him.

Q&A
Repeat and Reframe
Answer the Questioner
Widen
Look for the next

The first strategy is to repeat the question. The questioner might not have a microphone, and the speaker probably does. This allows time to think and lets everyone in the room understand the question clearly. It also allows the speaker to check with the questioner that the question has been understood. In some cases, it allows the speaker to slightly reframe the question to be more applicable to the audience or easier to answer. Once that's done, the speaker initially addresses the questioner, gradually widening the answer to include the whole room, leaving the questioner behind (discouraging follow-up questions), and looking around for the next question.

The second strategy is that the speaker should not be afraid to take the conversation out of the room. "That's a great question, but I'd like to talk to you in greater depth than we have time for here" allows the speaker to remove a grandstander, avoid discussing topics that are irrelevant to the audience, or avoid talking about things that should be kept confidential.

Third, it's important to remember that it's quite OK to say "I don't know." This is fine if you offer to find the answer and follow up with the questioner later. Of course, you really *must* follow up later.

I was awarded "favorite husband" status when I took my wife to a film industry screening of the film *Ides of March*. The screening was followed by a Q&A with members of the cast, including George Clooney. My wife asked a question that Mr. Clooney answered, to her delight addressing his long answer to her directly and seemingly ignoring everyone else in the room. Like I said, these are not rules, just guidelines. You can ignore these guidelines as appropriate, particularly if you're George.

Step 10: Aftermath

My mobile rang at 10:45. Barry was whispering into the phone. He sounded slightly drunk.

"I'm in the foyer; I don't know what to do."

I asked how the presentation went.

It was fine, and he'd returned to his seat but felt unable to stay in the auditorium.

I felt he needed permission. I gave it.

There's a phenomenon I call *horizon blindness*, which afflicts many who work in the event business. I suspect anyone who is project based must have the same problem. We start out working on something that is three months away and carefully schedule resources to achieve the goal. As we work through the project, the goal becomes two months, six weeks, three weeks, ten days, five days, seventy-two hours away...and so on.

We think about nothing other than the looming deadline, which becomes ever more present until we get past the end of the project and feel slightly bemused because the process has continued as the deadline approaches: 12 hours, 6 hours, 90 minute, 30 minutes, 5 minutes....

At the end we have to face what we are going to do with the rest of our life, and it's a bit of a shock to the system.

Also, if, like me, you are an introvert, giving the presentation is—with practice—the least part of the problem. The coffee break afterward when everyone wants to speak to you is a real shocker.

Barry wasn't prepared for his feelings after the presentation. I told him to go for a walk, take 45 minutes to walk around the block a few times, and be back in time for the next break—which was scheduled for noon.

I knew there would be people asking to speak to him. After all, that was the objective. He had business cards ready. I told him he should aim to be as transactional as possible. Swap cards, agree to talk again, and move on to the next person. Focus on those people from overseas and set a time to talk to them immediately. Everyone else he should arrange later.

I then gave him the rest of the day off.

I don't know what his boss might think about that, but I knew he'd be useless anyway.